FRAGILE GEOMETRY

The Films, Philosophy, and Misadventures of Nicolas Roeg

FRAGILE GEOMETRY

The Films, Philosophy, and Misadventures of
NICOLAS ROEG

by

JOSEPH LANZA

PAJ PUBLICATIONS
NEW YORK

Library of Congress Cataloging in Publication Data
Fragile Geometry: The Films, Philosophy, and Misadventures of Nicolas Roeg
Library of Congress Catalog Card No.: 87-73283
ISBN: 1-55554-033-3 (cloth)
ISBN: 1-55554-034-1 (paper)

Printed in the United States of America

Publication of this book has been made possible in part by grants received from the National Endowment for the Arts, Washington, D.C., a federal agency, and the New York State Council on the Arts.

for
Billy Halop
1920-1976

ACKNOWLEDGEMENTS

Special thanks to David James, Robert Littman, Rick McCallum, Paul Mayersberg, Adam Parfrey, Theresa Russell and Allan Scott.

Also to Richard Combs, Paul Drake, Jillian Hartnoll, Andrea Jette, Francisco Mattos, Lewis Shoenbrun, Zita Siegel, Jim Vinson, and all of my other friends and associates who have assisted me with knowledge, supplies, photographs and occasional resuscitation.

And, of course, gratitude to my partner in crime, Nicolas Roeg, for offering his private collection and generous time.

Stills courtesy of Almi, Cannon Films, Island Alive, Island Pictures, David James, Carolyn Jardine, Lord Snowdon, Peter Lyster-Todd, WW Entertainments, MGM/UA, Paramount Pictures, Warner Communications and Twentieth Century-Fox.

CONTENTS

ROEG AS A NOEL COWARD-STYLE YOUTH

NICOLAS ROEG

INTRODUCTION

NICOLAS ROEG IS ON THE VERGE OF GOING MAD—A fact which he proudly acknowledges and which his films invariably expose. Far from being a handicap, this vacillation between lunacy and sobriety makes him one of our most brilliant and exasperating directors. Being *on the verge* is intrinsic to Roeg's creative process. His films are orgies of ambivalence that ogle us neurotics who prefer to flirt with the abyss rather than topple into it.

"Hypnotic," "pretentious," "complex," "visionary," "perverse," and other epithets credited to or leveled against him demonstrate Roeg's immunity to neutral reactions. Such notoreity may stem from the fact that Roeg simultaneously embodies film's pinnacle and its nemesis. His work is the progeny of an expert craftsman and problematic storyteller who eschews the slickly-assembled movie for something much more risky. This is why, in all of his films, a serious foray into the seamy side of human character can suddenly turn into a disarming joke, or a surreal landscape may clash with a more conventional genre to prevent recourse in reason or escape in absurdity.

Roeg's stylistic complexity and open-ended intentions are crucial to his subject matter. When we try to explore the meanings of love, death, ecstasy, despair, mysticism, and the perplexities of psychic and physical space-time as obsessively as he does, we are bound to emerge from the pilgrimage more discombobulated than we were when we began. *A pursued gangster undergoes an identity transformation after meeting up with a disillusioned rock star; an architect in Venice is haunted and finally immolated by his dead daughter's specter; a space alien falls to earth, starts a multimillion dollar enterprise and is later imprisoned and mutilated by a mysterious government-corporate collusion; or a couple attempts to compress decades of married life into a single year on a deserted island, only to face estrangement and even revulsion toward one another.* These are just some of the Roeg scenarios which, even by their sparsest descriptions, divulge alienation and incongruity.

Roeg's relationship with his craft is one of love and war, a constant struggle between the sentiments he may intend to present and the contrary responses he often draws from audiences. He essentially perfects the self-consuming camera—a device engineered to fall back on its artifice no matter how its operator tries to depict "reality." This is an infuriating paradox similar to that of the quantum scientist whose subatomic world gets fuzzier as his instruments get more specialized and he focuses harder. The deeper Roeg attempts to probe beneath uncovered truths, the more the mechanism gets in his way. Ironically, this dilemma is his strength, the mating call that lures inquisitive viewers into his romance with dementia which, to our horror and delight, must never go beyond extended foreplay.

PRECISION & DELIRIUM

Mondrian & Muzak

In an existence of the hyphen, it is
impossible to be either wrong—or right.
—Charles Fort, *Wild Talents*

IT IS NO WONDER THAT MY FIRST ENCOUNTER WITH
Nicolas Roeg is in a place as visually overwhelming and thematically
oppressive as the restaurant of a hotel decorated in homage to the artist Mondrian. This plastic ambiance of glaring primary colors, multiple mirrors, supercilious waiters, vintage Muzak and other tokens
of high-class kitsch forbidding any kind of intimacy, is the necessary
ingredient to bring us to reality's tether—the meeting ground on
which Mr. Roeg and I feel strangely at home.

When interviewed, Roeg seems quite comfortable in a nether-
world between order and chaos. He even talks like his films as he
ponders over the limitless shades of a single idea with fragmented
and often inconclusive bursts of insight. Jumping from topic to
topic, he implies a hidden connection between ostensibly incongruous subjects. He speaks visually, gesturing with his hands
and face, even occasionally leaping from his seat to act out a point.
Then there are those moments of tentative repose when he stares

out onto an invisible chimera and tries to concentrate on a thought
which threatens to slip out of reach at any second. His small build,
penetrating green eyes and wizened yet attractive visage comple-
ment a gentleman's aplomb. But while exceedingly responsive,
Roeg also betrays a genteel aloofness. In the past, he has described
himself as a man with few friends, who spends most of his time in a
half-dream state—a dark and lonely side which emerges intermittently between reflective and humorous moments.

Apprehending Roeg's thought patterns is similar to an act of
divination. Listeners may pick any word or more from his wayward
sentences to catch on to an idea with far greater meaning than
maybe even he anticipates. Certainly in his own mental investiga-
tions Roeg seldom leaves a possibility unexplored. Each previously
unnoticed nuance in the surroundings can have a cataclysmic impact on a theme resonating in his highly absorbent brain. Even our
antiseptically tasteful table arrangement becomes a Roeg studio
prop, a reminder of how our decor and architecture are skillfully
designed not to entertain but to smother.

Roeg seems entrenched in a semi-aristocratic view of the world,
perceiving people as victims of abstract concepts like Destiny rather
than mundane social or economic conditions. He is more likely to
quote Nietzsche than Marx, less inclined to address the plight of the
working class and more content to use characters with ample to
plenty of money and obscene amounts of free time. Sometimes his
most casual observations ignore daily life's exigencies. From the moment we start talking, Roeg pulls me into his brilliant digressions
which give the illusion of more minutes passing by than he actually
allows. However, I start to wonder if this gnarled discourse is just
his clever way of throwing inquisitors off, conning them into
imposing their own meanings onto his open-ended agenda. But just
when I think that I may be lost, he taps my hand to assure me all is
well.

Periodically, Roeg interrupts to ask me how I am going to sort out
our circuitous idea exchange on my tape recorder. I also worry until
we finally disclose our mutual admiration for Charles Fort, the
legendary writer whose books such as *Wild Talents* and *The Book of
the Damned* ingeniously chronicle a taxonomy of strange facts
designed to be undermined by Fort's own subjective ruminations.
So, to circumvent any nagging copyright or legal problems, we both

agree that no matter how well the tape recorder processes our conversation, the meeting will become part fiction the moment it is transcribed onto paper. As the tapes disintegrate, we can only enter a quagmire where, as in Roeg's films, documentary struggles with dream.

* * *

ROEG: A strange thing happened to me. I ran into this screenwriter who gave me a story for a film which I thought absolutely wonderful, and he told me it was a joke. He said I could have it if I gave him $10.00.

What is it about?

I can't tell you, I'm afraid. It's such a brilliant idea. Then, he told it to someone else, and I said, "No! It's now MY story! I'M going to make this fucking movie!"

You're skillful and reckless at the same time, always drawing from unorthodox sources.

That's nice because it's there. A lot of it isn't made up. People usually go to the theater expecting something they already know about. I suppose life has become so surprising for everybody that they come to the movies not to be surprised but to be confirmed in their opinions. Cliché is what they look for. That's why the script Allan Scott and I worked on for *Castaway* had cliché already in there just so it would be more accepted. We had planned to take the cliché out once we began shooting.

Is that the first time you'd used that tactic?

Officially. Even the descriptions were cliché. We figured producers would be pleased, then shocked to find it absent in the final print. Life is certainly bizarre!

And uneven.

Yes, uneven. Life is constantly in flux, and it has become more so through the different mediums we're exposed to. It used to be fairly stable before the Industrial Revolution. Change came to the mind more slowly because it was by dispatch. We get information faster and to more places now. Life has become startling in its little tricks.

So, now people go to the theater for some sort of consistency.

Is that why most audiences prefer something action-packed?

Yes, I think so. They just want a momentary diversion. They don't want to leave a theater and say, "Where was I? My brain was taken away a bit." Nowadays, when people think their brain is being taken away, they reach for a gun and put up barricades. They say, "What's he doing to my head? He's fucking my brains out. My brains are fucked over enough as it is. The tax man's fucking my brains, my wife's fucking my brains, the kids are driving me crazy, now HE's driving me crazy!" When I first went to the movies as a boy, I believed everything I saw. The most extraordinary lives were happening before me, and mine was so mundane. I didn't want something that looked like MY life up there on the screen. I wanted the film to take me out of it. To make me think about something. Perhaps it's naiveté on my part, but I don't think a story of any kind can be simple. If you were to ask me to summarize my own life, I'd never be sure if I described it accurately. The past changes all the time for me. Finally, I come to the conclusion of never talking about it. Even if I described it exactly, I'd finally have to say it was not exactly that way. I think biography is probably more accurate than autobiography because a biographer is likely to think up fresher lies.

*   *   *

Nicolas: A Semi-Imaginary Portrait in Blue and Red

> *For with this desire of physical beauty mingled*
> *itself early the fear of death—the fear of death*
> *intensified by the desire of beauty.*
> —Walter Pater, *The Child in the House*

Nicolas Jack Roeg is born on August 15, 1928 to a Protestant household in London. He springs from a lineage of Dutch aristocrats who lose all of their money following World War I and must tolerate the rigors of middle-class existence. Nicolas's father, whose face is partially disfigured from the battlefield, spends most of his time unemployed and at home; while his mother, already of lower middle-class origins, toils in a bookshop. As Nicolas grows, he comes to admire his father's obsession with literature and his mastery of five languages, but (perhaps realizing the metaphorical import) cringes whenever the old man pulls him aside, looks into his eyes with an asymmetrical grimace, and reminds him that, ''You don't know how important it is to go through life with a tolerable face.''

The only childhood face Nicolas feels comfortable in presenting is that of a moody and dreamy boy forever miffed by the world's anticlimax. Only in his father's irregular countenance is he able to discern a beauty far superior to the regimented standards surrounding him. To make matters worse, financial woes force the Roegs to move from London to Brighton where Nicolas lives out his oppressive prep school days. It is, however, through his habitual strolls along the Brighton Beach seaside one summer that he experiences a near-fatal epiphany. The boardwalk's endless clamor of amusement rides, calliopes, sideshows and confectionary vendors embodies the last days of Britain's chaotic and crumbling empire. Nicolas perceives a disturbing beauty in this apocalypse and, in no time, converts it into a dreamscape of anemic, bloated and gnarled bodies squirming on blankets and in chaise longues, yearning to recoil from their evolutionary ascent and slither back to their primordial waters.

Each time Nicolas visits the beach, he reclines beneath his parasol, sips his lemonade and constructs the stages of this metamorphosis. The unflavored English scenery soon changes into a diorama of equatorial fauna and tropical insects whose hums induce intermittent numbness in the center of his skull. Coming home from one of these mental travels, Nicolas encounters his father peering at him from the window with that half-terrified, half-certain look of a parent all-too-familiar with his child's imminent awakening.

One day, while watching the crowds fidget with their tawdry paraphernalia, Nicolas gets impatient and fancies himself Cecil B. DeMille directing their ceremonial pilgrimage into the waves. The hovering clouds begin to resemble judgmental faces evaluating each sin as the throng of beachcombers await their redemption. The tangled flora along the palisades turn into mandibles gaping at the technicolor nexus where water and sky mate. For the first time in their lives, the sunbathers display a reptilian energy that had lain dormant for aeons. Pallid Anglo-Saxon complexions become bulbous and scaly. Their once weary and hunched demeanor now assumes the agile and chiropractically-correct gait of serpents intoxicated by the scent of brine. As the baptismal fluids draw them in, Nicolas is overwhelmed by the spectacle, but abruptly looks away before his fantasy gets too scary and its optical intensity induces a spontaneous cerebral combustion.

This is Nicolas's last visit to the seaside for a while, due to a sudden and mysterious illness. Pronounced fevers, frequent night sweats, migraines and occasional spells of glossolalia leave him immobilized in his cramped bedroom. His father listens outside the door to his son's frenzied but incomprehensible mumblings during the night. Nicolas is certainly somewhere else now, and anyone hoping to retrieve him intact hasn't a prayer.

Nicolas must ignore his severely limited confines by re-creating the ever-expansive beachfront in his mind. When the rest of the household sleeps, he shuts his eyes, and the epic rapture resumes. A childhood reverie transmogrifies into a convalescent's nightmare. No longer dignified souls waiting to be reborn, there are now dismembered pieces of viscera flailing and thrashing against the tide, unable to subsist on either water or oxygen. For a moment, he shifts his attention to the distant horizon's tranquil azure contrasting against the crimson froth of mutations and their oozing tentacles stretching from the shore back to the boardwalk. Eternity is out of reach. It's too late to go back. Nobody is saved. He wakes up screaming. A candlelit face looms over him. "The things you love are supposed to make your skin crawl," his father intones before blowing out the candle and leaving the room.

With every old world esthetic prejudice exorcised from his system, Nicolas is at last ready to return to his creations and accept whatever form they manifest. However, he is not well enough to leave home until summer's end. Debilitated from the extended rest, he barely manages to hobble back to the beach one late afternoon to find the attractions boarded up, the concession stands gone, and the loiterers back in school or at their jobs. He is the only one left to try and reconstruct the fragments. Looking out to the horizon of his dream, he finds the pale blue giving birth to a trace of sunset red—an emblem of the glorious cranial hemorrhage that might have been.

The Early Years
Serving Time in British Film's House of Detention

Roeg emerges from a generation wedged between two sensibilities as it gets to witness the radical technological and social changes capsizing the literary tradition by which it is reared. Hence, many of his film inspirations are literary figures, just as his cinematic innovations are riddled with allusions to the written word. We can also tap into his ideas about the nebulous nature of "truth" by considering some of the writers that leave the greatest impression on his developing mind. Besides Charles Fort, he admires a mélange of authors who totter between precision and delirium: Daniel Defoe, the chronicler of such events as Alexander Selkirk's shipwreck and the great "plague years," who, to this day, never assures us that he is telling the truth; Lewis Carroll, who atones for his mathematical acumen by composing tangled tales and hysterical whimsy; John William Dunne, the aeronautics wizard who, besides developing Britain's first military aircraft, draws some conclusions about time that are inimical to Euclidean stability. Of course, we cannot forget the notorious Walter Pater, our father of "aestheticism," who, more than anyone else, understands that the beautiful objects we revere are always doomed to crumble with our fleeting sense impressions.

Roeg's movie interests are already prevalent in his fledgling days at Mercers School, where he abrogates his raucous peer group activities to initiate film societies. The only other tie his family has to the entertainment world is the actress and Purple Heart winner Nicolette Roeg—his sister and close friend who encourages him to pursue the movie interests that his pedagogues consider aberrant. Roeg, in fact, seeks her guidance many times when trying to articulate some vagary he tries to inscribe in his journal. She is the first to call attention to his curious habit of relying more on gestures than words to explain a difficult concept, thereby revealing the tug-of-war between the hemispheres of his brain which never ceases.

In 1947, at the age of 19, Roeg gets his first career break when his father (who knows the owner) finds him a job at London's Marylebone Studios, where he fritters away at the De Lane Lea method of dubbing English dialogue over French films. It is here, amid the squalor and pedestrian rivalries of the postwar British industry, that Roeg becomes a kind of Walter Mitty, living out his drab apprenticeship while composing exotic scenarios in his head. The one film which truly affects him is Marcel Carne's episodic *Les Enfants du Paradis* with its inextricable melding of performers' lives with the somewhat more real events on the stage. (It will later be one of the many inspirations behind *The Man Who Fell To Earth.*)

During this period, Roeg's other cinema role models are British director Michael Powell and Powell's screenwriter Emeric Pressburger. Powell and Pressburger are British film's flower and thorn during the 1940s. Their sense of rich color and complex narrative keeps audiences spellbound, yet arouses significant ire because of the manner in which they push their skills into dangerous new areas that violate commercial decorum. During and shortly after the war, the industry is entrenched in social realism and does not appreciate Powell's unorthodox mixture of realist, romantic and supernatural themes. *The Life and Death of Colonel Blimp* is a fine example of Powell's tendency to tell a story through layers of flashbacks and flashforwards that disorient many viewers. *Black Narcissus* relates the identity crisis of a group of nuns when they enter a Himalayan landscape conceived entirely in a studio. Here the colors and the textures proudly override the plot. Then, his more popular *The Red Shoes* mixes ballet grandeur with fatalistic humor. Powell and Pressburger's exploits foreshadow Roeg's own career debacles since the British film establishment bestows a similar reception: praise for technical skill and condemnation for what is perceived as poor taste, flamboyance and lack of coherence.

After serving in the army with short stints as a still photographer and unit projectionist, Roeg returns to the cigar-toting studio world. In 1950, he gets to work at MGM's Boreham Wood Studios to serve as clapperboy for Hollywood veteran Joe Ruttenberg, the Director of Photography on H. C. Potter's *The Miniver Story*—a film praised by the masses for its quaint sentimentalism and later reviled by Gore Vidal in his novel *Myron* as a symbol of Hollywood's demise.

Roeg starts in an era when the business still gets many of its recruits through nepotism and suffers from a dearth of film schools to elevate the craft into respectable art. He even recalls a rather distressful time when the parents of a fiancée jeopardize his relationship by strongly disapproving of his career choice. However, he emerges from the trauma more convinced than ever that film is his true passion, even if this means being relegated to such unromantic duties as focus-puller on projects such as *Ivanhoe* and *Tarzan's Greatest Adventure.*

More promising tasks are in store a little later in 1956 when Roeg assists famed cameraman Freddie Young on George Cukor's *Bhowani Junction.* It is through his work with Cukor that Roeg becomes interested in the many ways the camera can create visual variety within enclosed spaces. Soon, he joins the crew on Wolf Rilla's *Pacific Destiny,* a film that features Roeg's wife Susan Rennie Stephen and his future star Denholm Elliott. (There is a quick shot of Stephen and Elliott from the film, right of center, among Newton's army of television sets in *The Man Who Fell To Earth.*) Among other memorable projects are Assistant Photographer for Ken Hughes's *The Trials of Oscar Wilde* in 1960, the same year that Roeg gets his first slam from scissor-happy editors who delete several of the Australian outback scenes that he helps to create in Fred Zinnemann's *The Sundowners.*

Perhaps Roeg's real escape from the fetters of technical servitude is aided not by the camera but the pen, when he co-writes, with Kevin Kavanaugh (who will later be Unit Manager on *Performance* and Assistant Director for *Walkabout*), the story for Cliff Owen's *A Prize of Arms* in 1961. Owen's film, about a group of thieves who attempt to pull a heist on the British Army, is notable less for its crime drama and more for its occult implications when one of the criminals has a vague premonition of events that ruins their plans. Disliked by some critics for its supposedly murky plot and incomprehensible cockney (charges later made against *Performance*), *A Prize of Arms* is too supernatural to be realistic and vice versa. Hence, Roeg makes his first entry into the maze of narrative paradox which, like an Escher moebius, gets more vertiginous and reflexive as the 1960s continue.

ROEG WITH FRANÇOIS TRUFFAUT AND JULIE CHRISTIE
ON THE SET OF *FAHRENHEIT 451*

THE PSYCHEDELIC WARLOCK

(1962-1968)

ROEG: It's amazing how nowadays everyone competes to talk the loudest. Women seem to be adopting all of the negative male traits. It's all part of the times—when no one, male or female, wants to be fragile or receptive.

Softness is among the things you most admire in people?

Well, if not softness, at least the ability to be at peace with yourself when your façade breaks down. In the sixties, the idea among many people was to relinquish the fortress and open up to the person next to you. Today, no one wants to give up their allotted roles. I guess it goes back to what we were saying about simple stories, doesn't it? People want their expectations coddled.

Do you feel out of place now?

No, not really. I've probably changed in some ways myself, although I still consider myself an old hippie. I'll always be attracted to the world of art nouveau, candles, incense, sensuality.

You continue to use many tried and true sixties techniques: the zoom, for instance. It's still a big part of your work, even though most directors avoid it today.

I can't forsake what excites me for current tastes. I want the camera to always be moving, even manic. To me, the zoom calls attention to the fact that the camera can go where the human eye can't. These days, the camera is often less obtrusive while the special effects get more elaborate. We are back to Georges Méliès with long shots and fancy gadgets in the background. Many of these new science-fiction films look like commercials for *Popular Science* magazine. That's why I often feel that the moon landing has hardened us a bit. We had conquered fantasy; so the only wonder left is in how elaborate we can make the hardware. I can remember being in Los Angeles during the Apollo landing. I couldn't believe I saw so much accomplishment confined to the tiny television frame. I was amazed and saddened because I thought that once we reached the moon, fact finally overshadowed fantasy. It will probably be years before we can anticipate visiting other galaxies.

Do you see movies as a fantasy medium?

I can't really say I know what that means. I hate the idea of so-called "dream sequences." It sounds patronizing, giving dreams secondary status. I'm more interested in the tension between what society considers "conscious" and how it feels when you know you're near madness. I'm afraid kids growing up now won't appreciate absurdity as much as the previous generation because the cartoons have become so literal. Children's programming is being monitored by adults now more than ever before, which is a shame. In the late fifties and sixties, parents tended to set their kids in front of the television just to get them out of their hair. Consequently, children were exposed to all kinds of zany and impractical role models, which may account for the wonderful exhibitionism they showed when they got older.

Timothy Leary warned against getting too polluted by psychedelic propaganda.

That's why I have reservations about translating drug experiences onto film. In *Performance* I kept it more simple. No light shows or strobes. Even the hallucinogen they used was not widely known at the time. It's hard to translate a drug experience on film without falling into cliché. Yet, probably our best fairy tales began with hallucinogens.

* * *

THROUGH THE 1960S, THE FILM MEDIUM BASKS IN A delightful decadence that makes the *film noir* era look conservative by comparison. This is a time when even the most self-proclaimed avant-gardists tacitly acknowledge the debt owed Walt Disney Studios for consummating the union of technical virtuosity with excess and bathos. Contrary to the unfounded opinion that the written form lags behind the visual, it is film that finally catches up with late Victorian purple prose or Marcel Proust's meandering thought patterns. Fellini, Antonioni, Resnais, Godard, along with smaller budget artists such as Warhol and Anger, flout Hollywood slickness with a frenzied métier that stumbles over its convoluted syntax. The director's director blossoms as filmgoers reach for their arsenal of anti-expectations. The very state of disorientation signals a vigilance for deeper meanings. It is, likewise, up to us to get over our petty discomforts and pretenses to "common sense" and somehow make conceptual peace with this flickering pandemonium. As Director of Photography, Roeg glitters in this atmosphere.

Roeg's cinematography and other camera work captivate and shock us with his use of light, color, angle and montage to alter a story's context or to evince the hidden beauty in things ordinarily considered uninviting or repugnant. He accurately captures the contrived dazzle of film at its pressure point. Even in less notable projects as Robert Lynn's *Doctor Crippen* (with Donald Pleasence portraying the infamous physician on trial for poisoning his wife), Roeg proves his talent for subtle lighting and camera acrobatics to add texture to an otherwise stagey production. Then, again in 1962, with Clive Donner's film of Harold Pinter's *The Caretaker,* he accents the odd triangle between the two brothers (Robert Shaw and Alan Bates) and the old man (Donald Pleasence) with skulking camera and creeping shadows. The expert handling of claustrophobic space (later refined in *Performance* and *Insignificance*) is already alive here with most of the action transpiring in a cluttered Hackney attic. Pinter's dialogue is even more disconcerting when complemented by photographic ventures through doorways and at curious vantage points that distort each character's bearing. The most notable example occurs towards the end when the camera circumnambulates around Robert Shaw as he recounts an ordeal in a mental institution.

In 1964, after playing 2nd Unit Cameraman for David Lean on *Lawrence of Arabia*'s trainwreck sequence and writing the initial script for Lawrence Huntington's *Sanders* (a photographically flawless but relentlessly uncinematic remake of the 1930s film *Sanders of the River* about diamond smuggling and murder in Africa), Roeg celebrates his next big project with a bacchanalia. Roger Corman's adaptation of Edgar Allan Poe's *The Masque of the Red Death* reveals Roeg's obsession with ensanguine settings foreshadowing *"Don't Look Now"* (Corman's film even begins with a specter in a red hood). Roeg's technique now begins to emit rhetorical ironies by making the evil Prospero (Vincent Price) the more glamorous character amid a lavishly photographed masked ball inside of an opulent castle. There are harbingers of *Eureka*'s voodoo sequence with Prospero's wife (Hazel Court) sacrificing herself in an elaborate Satanic rite and, of course, the masked ball in the King Zog sequence in *Aria*. During production, Corman even interrupts his manic shooting schedule to laud Roeg's unforgettable tracking shot of Francesca (Jane Asher) walking through a series of different colored rooms, which predates the famous scene in *The Man Who Fell To Earth* when a waiter wheels a cocktail trolley through the halls leading to the incarcerated alien.

In 1965, Roeg has a supposed row with David Lean, halting his seven-week preparations to photograph *Doctor Zhivago*. However, he makes up for the loss that same year on his first collaboration with long-time friend Richard Lester as cinematographer for the movie version of Stephen Sondheim's musical *A Funny Thing Happened On The Way To The Forum*. This is a project in which Roeg also does some uncredited last minute screenwriting, prompting Lester himself to publicly praise his partner's ''good script sense.'' His signature is most prominent in the film's studied incongruities and anachronisms. Ancient Rome is presented with vibrant colors and blonde female harems filmed through tinted filters and depth of focus shots to create what looks like a sixties fashion ad. But this technique of using a photographic style that does not quite go with the time period continues one year later with François Truffaut's *Fahrenheit 451*.

Fahrenheit 451 is the first science-fiction film designed to make the audience feel like the aliens. It is, in many respects, Roeg's first directorial effort since it has all of the innovations and pitfalls for which he is renowned. Besides having a big hand in the production, he also manages to supply us with many of his estranging habits:

surreal color schemes, deliberate pacing jarred by sudden jump-cuts, people and objects photographed off-center and the bizarre tendency to give a disproportionate amount of narrative time to explore relationships between emotionally uninviting characters. It is even stranger that someone like Truffaut (known mostly for his cozy, humanistic love stories) directs a film that is so icy, undefinable and structurally ambivalent.

Taken from Ray Bradbury's tale, *Fahrenheit 451* presents a society where books are banned and burned by an elite army of firemen, one of whom is the main character Montag (Oskar Werner), whose coming of age the story centers around. In the beginning, Montag is the model citizen who accepts his social taboo and, with his wife Clarisse's (Julie Christie) prompting, concerns himself only with his next promotion. His life soon alters when he meets and falls in love with Linda (also played by Julie Christie), who operates an underground library and persuades Montag to re-evaluate his identity and the laws that define it.

Montag's confusion is a starting point for the film's self-consciously bewildered look. There is also the story's premise which sets up a barrier between the written and visual medium and then proceeds to obscure the distinction. This may explain the constant conflict between poignant imagery and stodgy dialogue. While the camera distracts and makes us wonder what and why we are watching, the non-visual elements still get in the way. Truffaut scratches through the surface of Bradbury's story to expose its implicit absurdity, as pictures and words assume a figure-ground illusion whose contrasts alternately overshadow each other. In one scene, after the firemen stage a book-burning raid, a Salvador Dali catalogue ignites page by page—the word and image finally indistinguishable in the biblioclast's eyes. The characters' (especially Montag's) somnambulent speech and behavior are well in keeping with the film's purpose to make the performers two-dimensional artifacts waiting for words to vivify them.

As a result, the whole movie is predicated on inverted logic: the firemen slide up poles instead of down, start fires instead of putting them out. Roeg's photography tempts us into being the villain's passive accomplices. The arsonist exploits become the film's most visually captivating moments, making this the first Roeg effort to officially raise the ethical questions about the gulf between his possible intentions and his final effects. How are we supposed to feel when our visual fascination conflicts with our emotions? What is the film-maker's (or cinematographer's) true viewpoint? How much is meant to be serious, and how much is a sardonic joke? *New York Times* critic Bosley Crowther uses these questions as artillery:

> It's hard to believe that Mr. Truffaut could be guilty of such poor taste. Poor writing, yes, and dull direction, but certain-ly not poor taste! He wouldn't dare put into a picture in-tended to be a joke a scene so ugly and currently evocative as one of a captured booklover setting herself on fire. . . . No, it strikes me that Mr. Truffaut got himself tangled up with an idea that called for a slashing satire beyond his grasp.

Reaching beyond one's grasp, in this case and in later Roeg endeavors, may or may not be a fixed purpose. *Fahrenheit 451* is among few films to open itself up to us with both grandeur and humility, asking us to complete its meaning while bombarding us with too much to interpret. *Variety* claims that, in this film, "too often the spectator is left on the sidelines and neither convinced by nor accepting what is projected on the screen."

Even *Fahrenheit 451*'s time period is tentative. In *A Funny Thing Happened On The Way To The Forum*, Roeg helps to make the past unrecognizable. But in the Truffaut film, Roeg reveals his interest in *chronocentric futurism*, coloring visions of past and future with present-day trappings. To achieve this, Truffaut judiciously gives Roeg and set designer Tony Walton *carte blanche* in their efforts to devise scenery that is creepy and ridiculous— Orwell's *Nineteen Eighty-Four* transposed onto *Babes In Toyland*. The firemen wear Buck Rogers-style uniforms and fly around in rocket-lift devices. Many scenes are dominated by a parody of the Disneyland monorail. Though the homes are futuristic enough to have giant video screens transmitting daily indoctrination, they also display the familiar details of sixties suburbia with roofs cluttered by TV antennae and immaculately mowed lawns. Roeg claims: "When we discussed the film, he (Truffaut) said, 'I don't want it to have a reality. I want it as a Doris Day film, with little shining colors.' He wanted a certain sense of awkwardness in behavior patterns."

After *Fahrenheit 451*'s stylistic mayhem and subsequent critical bafflement, Roeg gains a reputation for his charming and offending eye. He becomes more dexterous and subtle in the art of defamiliarizing, pulling us into each film only to distance us again. But while his growing popularity in movie circles opens him to lucrative offers, Roeg often poses commercial risks, even with films more suited to mainstream audiences. Such is the problem in 1967 when his photography for John Schlesinger's *Far From The Madding Crowd* engenders considerable controversy. Here, Roeg collaborates on a rather chancy interpretation of Thomas Hardy's novel set in nineteenth-century Wessex. The film tells the story largely through the viewpoint of Bathsheba Everdene (Julie Christie), the female protagonist whose various loves stir up hostilities in a rural community. There is an unusual sensitivity to the environment, a reception to color and scenery that often interferes with the plot mechanisms. Intense tones set against bluish-gray backgrounds give the film a surreal glow working counter to the supposed pastoral setting. There is also a lackadaisical pacing that sabotages what promises to be a tale with a more linear progression.

Far From The Madding Crowd's awkward moments are probably due to its accurate adaptation of Hardy's own questionable realism. In the novel, the community speaks a peasant dialect, but the principal characters have a speech and vocabulary that is inexplicably aristocratic. Literary critic Terry Eagleton describes Hardy and his novel in terms that could also apply to Roeg:

> (Hardy is) the creator of "memorable" scenes and characters; yet he can be scandalously nonchalant about the "purity" of orthodox verisimilitude, risking "coincidence" and "improbability." With blunt disregard for formal consistency, he is ready to articulate form upon form —to mingle realist narration, classical tragedy, folk-fable, melodrama, "philosophical" discourse, social commentary, and by doing so to betray the laborious constructedness of literary production. (*Against the Grain*)

Some critics think the scenes are over-photographed and that the camera tends to linger too long on petty details. In her book *The English Novel and the Movies,* Rita Costabile dislikes how

humans and nature seem curiously indifferent to one
another . . . the intricate harmonies and dissonances which
characterize the exchanges between men and the world in
the novel have been blunted by an insistence on omitting
the dissonances and either overdramatizing or prettifying
the harmonies.

Far From The Madding Crowd also introduces us to Roeg's quasi-
feminist views on film narrative. Considering the "action" film too
much a vestige of boy's fiction, Roeg helps Schlesinger to adopt a
more contemplative and sensual approach favoring isolated thoughts
and moods over any clockwork progression of events. The film also
presents its story through understated climatic and seasonal changes
that convey a time passage without any direct chronological
references—a technique later exaggerated in *Walkabout, The Man
Who Fell To Earth, Eureka,* and to a smaller extent in *Castaway.* "I
think the film was underestimated," Roeg later laments. "It came
at a time of change. John tried to capture the feeling of seasons
through a rather leisurely pace—and it came at a time when cinema
audiences were accustomed to another sort of pace."
   If Roeg's artiness up till now elicits some wary responses, his next
effort, Richard Lester's *Petulia,* receives scorn from those who feel it
is too elliptical and distraught. *Petulia* prepares us for *Performance*'s
even more crazed editing, a retinal rollercoaster ride fitting for its
theme of spiritually vacuous urban jetsetters during San Francisco's
acid heyday. Full of abrupt, near-subliminal crosscutting to suit the
characters' fragmented psyches, *Petulia* also has a disjunct
chronology and preoccupation with the aesthetic appeal of operating
rooms that predates *Bad Timing.*
   Like *Far From The Madding Crowd, Petulia* is mostly preoccupied
with the feelings and impressions of its female lead. Julie Christie is
cast again, this time in the title role, as a *bon vivant* who, beneath
her chic exterior, is a manic depressive with a husband (Richard
Chamberlain) who beats her and a lover (George C. Scott) who cannot understand her. She is also burdened by a Mexican child hurt in
an auto accident after she, at her husband's insistence during a
domestic quarrel, reluctantly smuggles him over the Tijuana border.
The camera repeatedly reminds us of how Petulia's destiny is linked
to the young cripple with cuts to his accident and subsequent opera-

tion interspersed with scenes of Petulia's approaching emotional collapse.

There is a contrast between superficial fun and underlying sickness, the most memorable example being at the film's beginning when a wild psychedelic party is intercut with a group of invalids in a descending elevator. The juxtaposition quickens until it is clear that the cripples are on their way to the bash, thus preparing us for the final scene when Petulia is approaching her own convalescence on a hospital bed, calling out her lover's name before being anesthetized. Roeg's photography manages to capture the story's empty glamor. There is the recurrent motif, with Roeg's characteristic vagueness, of an orange light show that mysteriously pops up at various points as Petulia hallucinates.

The film gets one snide response from John Simon who calls it a "soulless, arbitrary, attitudinizing piece of claptrap." But Richard Schickel, who later lambastes *Performance,* credits *Petulia* as a "sad and savage comment on the ways we waste our time and ourselves in upper middle-class America."

Petulia is made the same year that Roeg and his perennial chum Donald Cammell collaborate on the film that spearheads Roeg's ecstatically hazardous directing career. Essentially, Lester's film provides a link between Roeg's sixties look and the more strident anti-narrative excursions to come.

ROEG WITH MICK JAGGER AND DONALD CAMMELL
ON THE SET OF *PERFORMANCE*

SHOUTING IN THE DARK

The Perils of Cinema's Hitman

ROEG: Many directors like to talk down to their audiences. That comes from expectations. To me, entertainment is something you are drawn into, an occasion to lose yourself. It has to do with what I said earlier about going to the movies to be confirmed in your aesthetic prejudices. Most of the time, people just want a little bit of distraction. They look at the screen and say, "Oh, that's pretty, but, oh shit, I've got to pay the tax bill. Oh, that's a nice scene, look at her big tits, but oh what am I going to do about the wife and kids and the doctor bills?" That's not being entertained! Technically, the seventies produced some great works—*Earthquake,* for instance, was astounding. But it's really hard for me to take a straightforward, linear film all that seriously anymore. It seems we've grown up now and don't need to be led by the hand.

How do you feel about our current George Lucas nostalgia school?

The only amazing thing about those stories are the effects, aren't they? It's a relief for audiences because they really don't have to get involved. You can't really feel for the Princess in *Star Wars*, can you? It's wonderful technically, but that's all. I guess it's escapism. It certainly doesn't help me to escape in any way. It just makes me realize all the more where I am.

The reactionary wave started in the seventies.

Right. But then it happened everywhere, didn't it? And just look at
where it led—something like the Reagan-Gorbachev Summit.
That's something, isn't it? I think it's wonderful. People seriously
read the total madness and nonsense. They actually take these
leaders as serious people. I think Johnny Carson is more serious
than Reagan and Gorbachev put together.

But wouldn't it make a great film?

Well yes, if they were forced to wear jester hats with dangling bells
instead of suits and ties. Then their Summit would be worth
watching. They'd look like absolute assholes. They'd never be able
to discuss anything. That's what politics really has become. Total
nonsense. It's not even worth reading about in the papers. But if
these serious media figures appeared in drag or something like that,
it would make so much more sense.

Why do you avoid putting politics into your art?

Because it's total rubbish, and I don't want it in any of my films.
Yet, one wonders what one means by ''politics.'' Politics to me is
all about trying to help the human lot, or to understand how people
relate to each other. In that sense, how could my films *not* be
political? Whether you're a Democrat, Republican, Tory or Liberal
finally makes little difference. It's just a job!

How about outwardly political directors like Bertolucci?

Actually, he's a wonderful filmmaker. But I believe that if you want
to put partisan politics into a film, it should be made by the political
party. Film to me is not a platform. If you leave a film feeling more
compassionate towards people and their frailties, then it has served
its purpose. Mao tried to have little red books, but no one really read
them. Who reads them now? I've been nailed about being apolitical
many times.

The Man Who Fell To Earth *has some political overtones.*

It was certainly about capitalism. Bernie Casey, the black actor in
the film, amazed me. I cast him because I wanted a black man to
have reached that total confidence that he was part of the American

establishment. There's still so much condescension in the air with people being over-polite to the black executive. But I wanted to go beyond that point. I told him I wanted him to be a retired Air Force colonel. In the scene where he talks with Buck Henry about taking over the Corporation, he was supposed to wear an executive's hat, but he refused. He ended up carrying it in his hand instead because he felt he would be compromised if he had to assume the complete pose. Now I consider that a much more interesting political issue than something silly like the Peace Summit, which is thought of as straightforward while my movies are thought of as elliptical. I think that is more elliptical than anything I could possibly conjure.

You don't like being labeled "obscure," do you?

No, I don't. I wish people would at least try to understand. When *Last Year at Marienbad* came out, all of these hard-nosed, rock-faced people would storm out saying Resnais didn't know anything about putting together a narrative. They couldn't accept an actor going upstairs in a blazer and coming downstairs in a dinner jacket. But in every commercial today, you see mommy putting a pie in the oven, then you cut to the kids eating it. No questions asked. People accept ellipticism more in other forms, but the cinema is so far behind.

I see Nicolas Roeg as a logical extension of what movies would have been like if the sixties experiments continued.

Directors are under intense pressure now. I can't blame anyone for bowing out. We live in reactionary times. When you take a big step forward, as we did in the sixties and early seventies, there's always that small step back. The reactionary wave has affected everything: films, literature, politics, computers, plumbing. This is the time of return. There's a natural cycle that goes into decay. I thought this current trend would just take three or four years, but we are now stuck in a ten-year cycle. Those in the advanced camp will find themselves in back of the line tomorrow. As for me, I'm just getting by.

* * *

JILTED BY STUDIOS, HOUNDED BY CRITICS, GELDED BY censors and dismembered by mystagogues, Roeg is among few directors to thrive so well under the gun. This is because he proves to be

an equally formidable marksman, a Luca Brasi of the cinema world
who prefers to disfigure narrative conventions prior to obliterating
them. In the process, he incurs often unearthly consequences, in-
viting notorious encounters and spooky synchronicities that further
blur the boundaries between the story proper and the mayhem
behind the camera.

The turbulent progression is partly due to the times in which
Roeg premieres as a director. By the early seventies, when *Performance* is released, the retrograde Coppola-Lucas-Spielberg mafia
diligently reduces the masses to the lowest common denominator.
Though films like *The Godfather, American Graffiti* and *Jaws* drag
us back to a mythologized past where movies are pure escapism,
Roeg and a few other mavericks play the pied piper by picking up
where beleaguered predecessors leave off. But Roeg does not commit
experimental *seppuku.* He instead remains a commercial director
meeting the conservative trend with a frontal assault, deploying
hackneyed stories and subverting them at the same time.

There is an uncanny parallel between some of the major seventies
films and Roeg's variant and subsequently less understood works.
When *Performance* appears, viewers are more than likely bewildered
by the equation between organized crime and the business world.
Then *The Godfather*, which follows just two years later, pursues the
same concept and gets hailed as socially relevant. Notice also the
stylistic contrasts between *"Don't Look Now,"* which treats the
occult with arcane references and ambiguous plot and William
Friedkin's *The Exorcist* with its simple storyline and garish pro-
sthetics to sustain the audience's attention. A few years later, *The
Man Who Fell To Earth* turns the science-fiction film on its head by
replacing predictable space adventures with an approach that is more
subtle and less defined. It, however, gets upstaged a year later by
Star Wars's computerized revival of futuristic hardware and boorish
distinctions between good and evil reminiscent of serials from the
thirties and forties.

Notwithstanding Hollywood's fashionable recidivism, the 1970s
are undervalued for structural innovations that come from the
fringe, not only in film but in literature. At this time, the ''open
text'' theories become popularized with Jacques Derrida's
''deconstruction'' doctrine, Hans-Georg Gadamer's ''herme-
neutics,'' German reception theory, reader-response criticism, and

other postmodernist covens turning narratives into a breeding ground for endless and never conclusive interpretations. We get closer than ever to perceiving a film's creator as just part of a nexus shared with the equally, if not more, important viewer. In fact, viewers and moviemakers become increasingly receptive as well as suspicious of each other's motives. Roeg's place in these trends is stridently, though pedantically, articulated in 1977 when *Sight and Sound* magazine publishes an article by Robert Phillip Kolker entitled "The Open Texts of Nicolas Roeg," in reaction to *The Man Who Fell To Earth*'s mixed appraisals. Kolker points out Roeg's experimental moxie which other filmmakers are losing. However, the one director most congenial to Roeg is Rainer Werner Fassbinder who also delights in letting artifice and seemingly extraneous details divert our attention from the core story. Like Roeg, Fassbinder is notorious for allowing genre pastiche and over-stylized drama to interfere with character empathy.

Roeg assaults conventions because he strongly believes that warring interpretations, even those rubbing against the creator's intent, are a movie's barometer of success. He lets the public know that he prefers to see the world through a camera whose viewpoint is misaligned. But it is not as if Roeg always prefers to bask in a director's chair with a stimulus-response regimen to calculate when and how audiences get disoriented or offended. He may sometimes just put together a story as his instincts demand, and the fact that audiences often do not "get it" can turn his iconoclastic endeavors into exercises in frustration.

PERFORMANCE

First reports of the killing spree begin in 1968, when Roeg and co-director Donald Cammell stand together hand-in-hand before the mirror one day and merge into that two-headed hydra whose offspring is among cinema's most brilliant aberrations. Twenty years since it first stalks the earth, *Performance* still thrives despite numerous attempts to have it dissected and surrendered to taxidermy.

Getting their initial inspiration from Vladimir Nabokov's *Despair*, which explores a man's fatal encounter with his alter-ego, Roeg and Cammell use the film as a sacrament for their own identity exchange. Roeg grows weary of the technocratic cinematographer's trade and Cammell is disillusioned with being a masturbatory artiste. There is no telling what kind of erotic, and even psychotic, encounter sessions they endure at each other's mercies, but they at least emerge from their self-imposed cloister with what Roeg likes to refer to as a "forehanded play," only half completed by the time shooting starts, with much of the story scripted and re-assembled as the film is made.

The credits list Roeg responsible for photography and Cammell for the story and script, but trying to break down exactly which director contributes what is fruitless since neither admits to *Performance* being anything other than a fifty-fifty collaboration. The re-invention of personality, Roeg's pet theme, materializes during the treatment phase. According to him, "The idea evolved from just a few pages that Donald had written—a notion for a film about a gangster in London's underworld, and the relation of that specific kind of violence to the violence in human nature."

Performance has obvious Roeg peculiarities: the jumbling of time, arcane visual metaphors, deliberate miscasting, subordinate characters with understated importance, books and other allusions displayed to tease us with deeper meanings, and a preoccupation with androgyny more overt here than in subsequent works.

The film follows the last days of Chas Devlin (James Fox), a young London gangster who gets so carried away with histrionic sadism that he torments Joey Maddocks (Anthony Valentine), a former lover who is also a recent, though reluctant, convert to the mob's takeover operation. The tension between them culminates in a quasi-sexual bloodbath when Joey and two thugs attack Chas in his flat, after which Chas shoots Joey in retaliation. The mob's chief, Harry Flowers (John Shannon), is perturbed by Chas's clumsy stunt, especially after warning him to "keep personal relations out of business" and orders his slaughter. Feeling the heat, Chas hides out in the home of an epicene ex-rock star named Turner (Mick Jagger) who lives with two ultra-psychedelicized women, Pherber (Anita Pallenberg) and Lucy (Michele Breton).

Using the alias "Johnny," Chas tries to pass himself off to the threesome as a "juggler" and finally persuades them to rent their basement apartment. Chas is of a conservative nature; initially appalled by the "freak show" of "long hair," "beatniks," "druggers'' and ''free love'' around him. But soon he is drawn into the osmotic web as Turner and Pherber tear into his repressed personality. With the aid of fly-agaric mushrooms (fed to him without his knowledge), Chas discovers a ''little dark mirror'' within himself that superimposes Turner's image over a dwindling macho persona. Chas recognizes Turner as his doppelganger and ''grim reaper'' while Turner, equally intrigued by the other's ''act,'' draws Chas further into a pansexual tryst. Meanwhile, the clocks of the putative ''real world'' keep ticking as Harry Flowers's gang eventually converges on the psychedelic sanctum. Then, before Chas gives himself up, he bids Turner goodbye, but (by some oracular impulse) shoots him in a similar manner he shot Joey, this time perhaps out of love instead of hate, or even for last minute loyalty to his clan to prevent Turner from talking.

One zealous rock critic describes *Performance* as a ''metaphysical comic strip.'' It is certainly among the few ''trip'' films to be salvaged from the LSD era without looking hopelessly dated. This may be due to its cynical approach that appeals to an emerging flock of embittered burnouts. The film also manages to expose the thin barrier between mind-expansion and mindfuck that so many acidheads inadvertently but routinely cross. Here is the movie that offers brutal assurance that life goes on, even if it resembles what most people dread seeing when they are chemically altered.

Besides being a swansong to the 1960s, *Performance* also heralds the onslaught of bisexual chic, much welcomed at a time when generic heterosexualism runs out of salable screen permutations. Along with films like Harold Prince's *Something For Everyone* and Bob Fosse's *Cabaret*, *Performance* is a healthy by-product of the new psychosexual breakdown. Though no stranger to gender-bending, Mick Jagger uses this occasion to exacerbate teenage sexual insecurities, accentuating the bitchy mannerisms and fellatio-crazed lips. While, at least by today's standards, its treatment of homosexuality seems too demure and evasive, *Performance* elicits panic which still reverberates in theaters generations later whenever audiences breathe that disingenuous sigh of relief as the person Chas kisses turns out not to be Turner but Lucy, whom Turner is made to resemble. It is also interesting to note that another film of that period to get equally undeserving barbs is Michael Sarne's *Myra Breckinridge*, whose dildo-toting transsexual commits another unprecedented assault on the masculine image. Besides its theme, *Performance* is one of the first films to self-consciously androgynize its structure with the brutal, choppy editing of the beginning sequences at South London, contrasted with the more distended, sensual narrative that unfolds at Turner's Notting Hill Gate mansion.

From its inception, *Performance* is a hellish ordeal. While assembling it, Roeg and Cammell are barred from their film lab after one of the personnel, shocked by clips appearing on the daily rushes, forces them to literally cut it on the outside pavement with the blade of a fire axe. When finally finished, it is shelved, due to the hysterical assumption that the public is not yet ready for it. Then, two years later, when Altamont and the Manson family saga expose psychedelia's livid underbelly, Warner Brothers assents, expecting to cash in on Jagger's newfound appeal as Satan incarnate.

Many of *Performance*'s nasty and moronic critical responses reveal it as a film both centered in and ahead of its time. In *The New York Times*, John Simon officially declares war on Roeg by putting *Performance* in his arbitrary "loathsome film" category, adding a snide remark about how the "smell of vomit" at New York's Waverly Theater (where it has a first run) reveals the appropriate audience response. Roeg develops a particular love-hate regard for Richard Schickel's *Life* review, which deems *Performance* a "completely worthless" harbinger of aesthetic decline. Roeg even carries a copy of it around with him as a memento mori and comic relief. The British critic Alexander Walker (who becomes another of Roeg's adversaries) claims that the movie "changed people from relatively reasonable individuals into impassioned denouncers of the evil they claimed it represented." A preview audience in Santa Monica reportedly gets disgusted enough to stage a mass exodus from the cinema. The MPAA, still breaking in its rating system, puts a damper on any anticipated teen appeal by branding the film with an "X."

Even those associated with *Performance* have misgivings. Warner Brothers, worried over a possible stigma, considers dumping it onto a smaller distributor. Roeg's agent frets over a possible lawsuit for "lack of professionalism"—a clause actually written into his contract. Rumors circulate that James Fox is skittish about being filmed in bed with Jagger and is later burdened by so much post-production guilt that he suspends his acting career to preach the Gospel. (Fox

later admits in his autobiography that this is his best role.) To make
matters even worse, a person on the camera crew has the temerity to
complain that the water in the bathtub sequence is too dirty.

After being cut and rearranged by at least seven different editors,
Performance looks like a ragged and rejected debutante at a coming
out party. Years later, Warner Communications abuses it even more
when releasing it on video with several unnecessary cuts, including
the important scene when Chas momentarily changes into Turner
after the first murder.

With *Performance*, Roeg acquires an amusing reputation for
wielding some kind of demonic influence over his actors and crew.
The monster is unleashed but once the shock diminishes, the prig-
gish and bigoted responses do *Performance* more good than harm,
providing the talisman that elevates certain films from box office
lepers to cult classics.

WALKABOUT

Roeg's next (and essentially his first) feature, *Walkabout*, is much
more accessible and less threatening than *Performance* but still incurs production and distribution snags. He is prepared to shoot the
film just after photographing *Petulia*, but the company supposedly
financing the production thinks Edward Bond's pithy script (65
pages in original draft) is too sparse and postpones. Bond, whose
previous contributions include a drama in a similar vein called
Saved, as well as English dialogue consultation for Antonioni's
Blow Up, caters to Roeg's need for a script that remains poetic (with
several lines composed in blank verse) yet open to numerous visual
interpretations.

Roeg intends *Walkabout* to be his "passion picture," harnessing
a complex tale of human survival and suffering in a simpler
framework that adults and children can enjoy. Based on James
Vance Marshall's novel, the film follows a young Australian girl
(Jenny Agutter) and her little brother (Roeg's son, Lucien John)
stuck in the outback. They are eventually saved by an aborigine
(David Gumpilil) on his "walkabout" or journey into manhood.
The three characters trek through the often sinister terrain and
become alienated by cultural differences—a rift made even wider
when the girl spurns the aborigine's affections. As the white

children grow more restless and yearn to return to Sydney, the aborigine loses faith in his tribal mission and, upon seeing an invasion of white mercenaries, stages an ominous ritual that leads to, what we can assume to be, his self-immolation.

Roeg's conception is decisively different from Marshall's. The novel has the children survive a plane crash, whereas Roeg adds a characteristically macabre touch by having them escape from their father (John Meillon) who tries to kill them during a family outing but instead kills himself. Marshall also makes the aborigine's death clearly the result of physical illness while Roeg leaves the reasons open-ended. Could it be the slaughtered animals that make him give up his will to survive? A fear of the encroaching civilization? Or simply unrequited love? Here, Roeg gets interested in mysterious deaths through the influence of Georges Polti's *The Thirty-six Dramatic Situations*, a book that combines mythology and folklore to illustrate how all human experiences, on and off stage, conform to pre-ordained patterns that are limited in number. Roeg is particularly engrossed in the chapter about ''The Enigma,'' the riddle that only death can solve.

Bond's original script also undergoes changes and deletions. Roeg begins by removing the characters' names so that they resemble allegorical wanderers with no personal identity. The early outline also has more tensions between the wilderness and the outside city. For instance, after the little boy tells the aborigine a story, the first script specifies a cut to a plane flying overhead; then another cut to the plane's interior where a flight attendant, two elderly women and a young businessman ignore each other even though they rub elbows in a confined space.

As in *Performance*, Roeg acts as both director and cinematographer. However, for the first time, he employs Anthony Richmond for special photography. Richmond will go on to photograph Roeg's next three pictures and may be responsible for the more grainy, ethereal look in some of the stop-action sequences and telephoto close-ups, contrasting with Roeg's sharper lens.

While *Walkabout*'s critical responses are generally luke warm, the film manages to get another notable jab from John Simon who accuses Roeg of gussying up the subject matter for no clear purpose. *Variety* describes it as a ''tepid'' attempt at an adventure story. Though it is Roeg's shortest work, *Walkabout* still has bowdlerization problems. In most American prints, there is an inexplicable cut. While the children are hiking, the aborigine comes across a factory where other bush children paint miniature ceramic kangaroos. A white woman, one of the shop's proprietors, approaches the aborigine with sexual overtures. After shunning her offer, the boy rejoins the two white children as the woman looks on. This deletion detracts from the constant tension Roeg wants between the wilderness and the colonial society on the periphery. Without it, the other interlude with a horny Italian meteorology team seems out of place. The scene also strengthens the film's shaky sexual perspective since it adds the rejected woman as a counterpart to the young girl who later rejects the aborigine.

What is most amazing about *Walkabout* is the manner in which Roeg combines the callow talents of Agutter and his son with those of Gumpilil, who speaks no English and has to communicate with Roeg and the crew mostly through sign language. There is actually an offscreen debate about whether to use Roeg's son for the little boy role. Roeg is not enthused about the idea until producer Si Litvinoff convinces him that a familial intimacy might translate well onto the screen.

During the filming, Roeg grows intrigued by Luc's experiences: "It was apparent that what I was doing was too sophisticated for Luc since he could only deal with it on a day-to-day basis, which was fantastic. So, I wanted to make his private thoughts into a kind of documentary." He plans a film, which is never completed, called *Luko's Diary* as an adjunct to *Walkabout*. From its description, it could be a prelude to *The Man Who Fell To Earth*, only approximating a child's, instead of an alien's, mental processes as glimpses of insight without a linear context.

Before advancing to his next major brainchild, Roeg also experiments with another kind of stylistic incongruity. *Glastonbury Fayre* is a filmed documentary, of sorts, about an actual rock festival held in the early seventies. Again Roeg attempts to use an outdoor setting to explore internal thoughts. Here the camera becomes our own desperate memory by transfiguring this last remnant of sixties counter-culture into a legendary and mythic epoch. The film even stages a facsimile of a medieval fair with Arthurian overtones. Though Roeg does not take directorial credit, *Glastonbury Fayre*'s mixture of fantasy and fact is his unmistakable concoction. Com-

menting on the project, he explains how "fashion and generation
gaps . . . are irrelevant," accounting for his desire to depict conflicting time periods in a single setting. As in *Walkabout, Glastonbury
Fayre* reinvents a "real" landscape that seems both natural and contrived: life as a mismanaged terrarium.

"DON'T LOOK NOW"

> I phoned Nic Roeg from Florida after I had read the script of
> *Don't Look Now* and said that I wanted to sit down and talk
> to him about it. He said: "What do you want to talk
> about?" I replied with this long speech about how I felt that
> ESP was a positive part of our lives and therefore we should
> make *Don't Look Now* a more educative sort of film, that
> the characters should in some way benefit from ESP and not
> just be destroyed by it. Nic said: "That's not how I feel." I
> said, "Well, what do you feel?" and he just said: "What's
> in the script, do you want to do it or not?" I asked if we
> could talk about it and he said "No." So I said, "Well, if
> you want to put it that way, yes I do . . ." and I just went
> and obeyed orders and had a wonderful time.
>
> —Donald Sutherland quoted in
> *Julie Christie* by Michael Feeney Callan

Waking up one morning to a London that is warmer and sunnier
than usual, Roeg pulls down his window shade and almost vomits
after an attack of agoraphobia. "To hell with the outdoors," he
mutters to himself, relieved that his next opus takes place in the
mazy enclosure of Venice.

As always when his queasy stomach portends trouble, Roeg pulls
out his Thoth cards, that infamous Tarot deck that the late British
warlock Aleister Crowley had designed to embellish and distort Kab-
balistic teachings. He shuffles the deck, spreads fifteen cards on the
bed and finds three of his favorite Major Arcana figures looking up
at him—the Tower, the Moon and the Hanged Man. The Tower
signifies quick and often catastrophic change. The Moon evokes
dark forces and delusion. Most important, however, is the Hanged
Man, a sign of sacrifice or death/rebirth by water. These three images will reel in his mind throughout his filming of *"Don't Look*

Now,'' Daphne Du Maurier's yarn about a couple haunted in Venice by the specter of their drowned daughter.

While in Venice restoring a dilapidated cathedral, John Baxter (Donald Sutherland) and his wife Laura (Julie Christie) meet up with two Scottish eccentrics: a blind woman named Heather (Hilary Mason) and her moody sister Wendy (Clelia Matania). Trouble brews when the blind woman claims to be a psychic who contacts the Baxters' dead daughter, Christine (Sharon Williams). Laura is virtually reborn from the revelation and makes a desperate attempt to use the sisters as mediums to reach the child. John, on the other hand, resists and gets even more skeptical when the clairvoyant also warns him that his life is in danger so long as he stays in the city. While doubting any psychic connections, John is nevertheless plagued by several ill omens: a near fatal fall from a cathedral scaffold; a forewarning of his own funeral procession; and fleeting glimpses of the homicidal dwarf (Adeline Poerio) who resembles Christine from a distance and rampages about the town, eventually luring him into a death trap.

With *"Don't Look Now,''* Roeg shows his ability to present glamorous perversions that even middlebrow audiences can explore. It stays faithful to Du Maurier's plot but is stamped with the director's peculiar signature. The entire film is dominated by red and blue tones, a visual melding of fire and water to which the Tarot's Tower and Hanged Man correspond. Roeg also seems to incorporate Crowley into his script's plot. In *The Book of Thoth* (Crowley's essay on Egyptian Tarot), one of the Hanged Man's descriptions is an aeon in which "all birth was considered an emanation, without male intervention, of the Mother or Star-Goddess, Nuit; all death a return to Her." Likewise, Laura Baxter and the Scottish sisters represent a matriarchal connivance working to exclude John from the hermetic death-birth process involving his daughter.

To make matters more sinister, Roeg laces the plot with a bevy of Hitchcock types: the half-phlegmatic, half-sinister Inspector Longhi (Renato Scarpa), the lugubrious Bishop Barbarrigo (Massimo Serrato) and an hysterical hotel proprietor (Leopoldo Trieste)—all of whom play their oblique role in the Baxters' misfortunes. The script, which Allan Scott had written along with Chris Bryant, is almost incantatory in parts, especially with the psychic, the Bishop and the Inspector, who intone their lines as if under an hypnotic trance.

Composer Pino Donnagio is an accomplice to the thaumaturgy with his crawly musical score.

One day during shooting, Roeg's mind wanders back to when he is on location for *Far From the Madding Crowd.* He recalls the augury of a white mare appearing on a grassy knoll that suddenly vanishes before he gets the chance to capture it with his camera. Interpreting this as an omen of innocence before catastrophe, he incorporates it into *"Don't Look Now"* 's opening scene when a white horse gallops across the Baxters' backyard while the daughter plays by the pond. (It will later reappear during a bucolic interlude in *The Man Who Fell To Earth,* again as a white unicorn in *Bad Timing* and as a carousel horse in *Track 29.*)

"Don't Look Now" 's critical response is, on the whole, much more positive. *Variety* calls it a "neatly-made, splendidly-acted . . . Superior, psychological thriller." There is, however, controversy over an explicit sex scene between Christie and Sutherland which some regard as both obscene and inessential. One sanctimonious quip emerges from London's *Daily Mail,* insinuating that Roeg is just out to titillate. Rumors also spread that an even more torrid version is made into a stag loop shown at chic Hollywood parties—claims which Roeg and Scott strongly deny. It is also important to remember that *"Don't Look Now"* is released in America just when studios contend with censorship problems resulting from a then recent U. S. Supreme Court decision making the definition of "pornography" subject to the whims of individual communities.

Annoyed by charges that the love scene is superfluous, Roeg actually deletes it in an experimental version. After watching it with as much objectivity as possible, he concludes that, without the scene, the story seems less engaging and the interim between the Baxters' last devoted moments together and their subsequent alienation in the wake of the sisters is left unexplored. Many who disapprove of the love scene also fail to realize that this is the Baxters' last intimate encounter before running into the hooded demon for the first time that same evening.

A few years later, in 1979, *"Don't Look Now"* returns to haunt Julie Christie. On her farm in Cefn-y-Coed in Wales, Christie discovers her friend Leslie Heale's twenty-two-month-old son drowned in a pond (in the same manner as the child in Roeg's film). With the black magician's mantle on his shoulders, Roeg must ask himself the question that *"Don't Look Now"* poses for us all along: Is it just an ugly coincidence? Or is some malevolent pattern evolving?

DEADLY HONEYMOON and OUT OF AFRICA

Apart from any inadvertent forces he may or may not be exercising, Roeg is also frequently the *recipient* of sadistic games, especially Hollywood's. The *Deadly Honeymoon* project is just one example. The novel and screenplay, written by W. D. Richter, involves two newlyweds who are accosted by, what appear to be, professional gunmen. After raping the wife and robbing the couple of their money, the thugs disappear. The couple, however, decides to take revenge. In their manic search, they gradually find themselves assuming the characteristics of the very people they are trying to apprehend. We later learn that the thugs in question are not even proper gunmen but impostors who take advantage of the couple's naiveté. And, in keeping with Roeg's endless obsession with people who always become what they most resist, the story concludes with the victims as victimizers and vice versa.

Looking forward to this project for some time, Roeg quickly arranges a shooting date and secures Jan Michael Vincent for the male lead. Then, just five days before filming is to begin, the MGM Inquisition summons Roeg to one of its dank luncheons. They inform him that the entire gambit is canceled. Roeg just looks down at his wilted Caesar's salad.

Shortly after this first MGM mishap, film history is gravely altered once again when Roeg's plans to direct Isak Dinesen's novel *Out of Africa* are also nixed. Already, with his work in films such as *Far From the Madding Crowd* and *Petulia*, Roeg demonstrates an affinity for exploring the female psyche, and in this project he has the perfect opportunity to investigate what he describes as ''the roots of womanhood, the nature of love and truth in relationships.'' The script he plans to use is written by Judith Rasko and is based on Judith Thurman's biography. Though it is the first script to win the Dinesen manse's full acceptance, David Begelman (who later plays a significant role in *Eureka*) is MGM's arbitrator at the time and pulls out of the project at the last minute, defending the decision with the usual backslapping and bureaucratese.

DAVID GUMPILIL, JENNY AGUTTER,
AND LUCIEN JOHN IN *WALKABOUT*

DONALD SUTHERLAND AND JULIE CHRISTIE IN
"DON'T LOOK NOW"

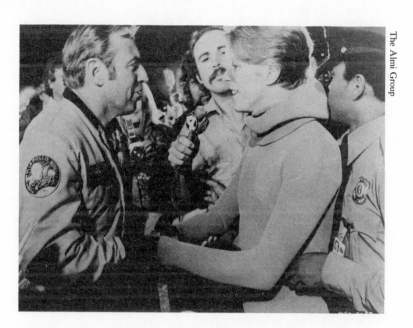

DAVID BOWIE WITH ASTRONAUT CAPT. JAMES LOVELL IN
THE MAN WHO FELL TO EARTH

THE MAN WHO FELL TO EARTH

Despite recent foibles, Roeg is surprisingly undaunted about delving into something as multifarious and risky as *The Man Who Fell To Earth*. The novel of the same name is written by Walter Tevis (one of his books appears in a *Fahrenheit 451* fire scene), whose previous works include the original story for the film *The Hustler* (later rehashed into *The Color of Money*). Before Roeg takes it on, *The Man Who Fell To Earth* is turned down three times: as a low budget TV movie of the week, a pilot for a television series and a feature presentation. Roeg courts Columbia Pictures for sponsorship, but the knotty script and David Bowie's dubious star potential are rejected. Finally, British Lion accepts the film as an act of faith, despite the fact that it is the first British movie financed solely by a British firm but shot exclusively in the United States with mostly American actors.

A space alien, who calls himself Thomas Jerome Newton (David Bowie), arrives one morning in a New Mexico town called Haneyville. By selling a large supply of gold rings he presumably brings with him, he accumulates enough capital to employ a lawyer named Oliver Farnsworth (Buck Henry) to patent the formula for a self-developing picture film. After marketing the product, Newton eventually forms World Enterprises—a vast corporation with himself at the top and Farnsworth the executor. This enables him to mobilize an energy conservation program to help him return to and save his drought-stricken planet.

However, in the process of attaining his goal, Newton gets sidetracked. He falls in love with a puerile country girl named Mary-Lou (Candy Clark) and locks horns with Nathan Bryce (Rip Torn), a scientist who joins the Corporation after being disillusioned as a high school teacher. Bryce's curiosity about his job's purpose and Newton's motives soon turns into suspicion. Newton's fling with Mary-Lou degenerates into middle-aged sadomasochism. He also exposes his identity to her while Bryce finds out through an X-ray he takes while Newton is unaware. As expected, Bryce conspires with the authorities who are already carrying out a clandestine plan of their own to clamp Newton's expanding power. The government-corporate collusion finally sabotages World Enterprises, liquidates Farnsworth and incarcerates Newton just before he makes his televised launch back home. Newton then undergoes a torturous series of tests and a lengthy imprisonment before being mysteriously set free to live the rest of his life as a dispirited alcoholic who still entertains the feeble prospect of returning to his dead family.

Even more than *Performance*, *The Man Who Fell To Earth* has multiple meanings and trap doors that defy any tidy plot synopsis. Its dense texture is largely due to screenwriter Paul Mayersberg, whose practice of genre-scrambling and plot-warping prove perfect for Roeg's ends. Roeg and Mayersberg initially think that an adaptation will be easy since the Tevis book is so well organized. But the more they fathom its translation onto celluloid, the more blind alleys they encounter. Consequently, *The Man Who Fell To Earth* undergoes a maddening process of rewrites. At the same time that producers Michael Deeley and Gary Spikings demand a coherent script and schedule, Roeg wants to convey as many ideas as he can, regardless of how much they interfere with linear progression or parsimony.

The Man Who Fell To Earth's pre-production incidents are also wrangling. Peter O'Toole is the first choice for the alien's role. Then, by a lark, Roeg views a David Bowie promo short called *Cracked Actor* and is instantly enamored by the "thin white duke's" hermaphroditic grace. One day, Roeg arrives at the rock star's home to talk the matter over and, with wife Angela Bowie's reluctant permission, remains for several hours until David returns that evening. Bowie is at first reluctant because he perceives the script as another corny variation on Robert Heinlein's *Stranger in a Strange Land*. But Roeg persuades him by explaining that it is essentially a love story with a millennial collage of Americana as its backdrop. After the consultation, Bowie is sold on the idea and even threatens to compose the film's soundtrack. Roeg prudently decides on John Phillips for the music and is able to procure him in spite of their reported shoving match a few months earlier in a New York nightclub when Phillips fails to help Roeg find the film's female lead.

If left to its original plans, *The Man Who Fell To Earth* would be drastically different. During the scene when Newton and Bryce discuss the existence of interplanetary visitors, the early script calls for interspersed shots of ancient carvings, sculptures and landing strips purportedly left behind by extraterrestrials. Instead of having Newton psychically meld with Bryce via a Kabuki show, Mayersberg plans to have Bryce watch a movie called "Fellini's Rigoletto," filmed among the ruins of an abandoned launch pad. The references to Newton's mission are also much more conclusive and detailed than in the purposely evasive final version.

Perhaps one reason this film results in a more abstruse and subtle approach is due to Roeg's insistence on keeping the cast and crew in constant suspense. While those behind the scenes grow confused over the film's structure and leery of the incubus awaiting them in the cutting room, other oddities transpire. The cameras tend to break down for no ostensible reason. During a location shot near an Aztec ruin, Bowie supposedly gets seriously ill after ingesting a glass of milk that has a viscous substance swimming around inside of it. Roeg, known for his disapproval of actors talking among themselves on the set, is especially fastidious about making sure his two principals, Bowie and Clark, are always within his physical and mental reach. While Bowie's dilettante attention span is centered on numerology, Roeg's alleged affair with Clark becomes public knowledge during the months she accompanies him on the film's promotional tour.

Bowie's character Newton is probably the first of Roeg's creations (preceding those of Art Garfunkel, Rutger Hauer and Oliver Reed) to serve as extensions of Roeg's own personality—vulnerable, brooding and sometimes gentle men with affectations of aloofness coupled with a propensity for tragic lust. Alcohol consumption, another of Roeg's much touted habits, is Newton's primary nemesis, and the film's ubiquitous Beefeater Gin bottle may be one of the director's many autobiographical lures.

As a final product, *The Man Who Fell To Earth* consists of a circus sideshow excursion into the American wasteland, released just in time for the 1976 Bicentennial. Its contruction is so intricate that many viewers feel compelled to resolve their bewilderment by expressing a flat dislike. The American distributor, Cinema 5, even resorts to passing out leaflets attempting to summarize and explain the film to audiences as they enter the theaters. As Nigel Andrews, a *Financial Times* critic, puts it: "The problem with *The Man Who Fell To Earth* is that it contains enough ideas for six different films, and far too many . . . for one." John Simon pronounces another malediction by declaring it is "like all Roeg films, the blowing up of something simple or simpleminded into arrogantly bloated dimensions and purporting to be chock-full of hermetic truths merely awaiting their interpreters.'' But Richard Eder of *The New York Times* describes the film as ''beautiful science-fiction . . . A first-rate achievement.''

During *The Man Who Fell To Earth*'s release, Roeg's public persona is enigmatic and withdrawn. He in no way attempts to abate the audience's suspicions or perplexed responses, preferring to conduct himself like Andy Warhol, using Candy Clark as his superstar and frontperson. During a visit to New York, while staying at the Algonquin Hotel, Roeg has the hair-raising treat of encountering the immaculate John Simon face-to-face. When Clark somehow arranges a meeting between the adversaries, the situation is nothing short of Doppelgänger camp. Roeg fancies this the perfect opportunity to impress Simon (the self-appointed arbiter of ''good taste'') by purchasing the most expensive wine he can find, only to be nonplussed when the critic brings along one of the cheapest. Then, after exchanging some nervous small talk, the two of them pose together practically holding hands in front of an instamatic camera which surprisingly does not shatter the moment the shutter snaps.

While getting unenthusiastic responses from the general British public, *The Man Who Fell To Earth* suffers far worse abuse after landing in the clutches of American curmudgeons who put it through Roeg's most botched surgery procedure to date. These edits, some twenty-two minutes worth, may reveal more about the individual censor's proclivities than anything else. Donald Rugoff, who purchases the rights for $800,000, is a Cinema 5 representative skittish enough about the film's promise to conduct an absurd marketing gambit fitting for a Roeg script. Assuming a coterie of budding social scientists can arbitrate public standards, Rugoff chooses to preview the film to a group of Dartmouth University psychology students who, in turn, complete a questionnaire specifying which parts they would like to see removed. From this sampling, Cinema 5 proceeds to make the excisions.

Among *The Man Who Fell To Earth*'s missing segments are: Bryce having sex with two more of his students; an overhead shot of Newton and Mary-Lou sleeping as heavy breathing sounds emit from an invisible source offscreen (indicating that the watcher who witnesses Newton land is still following him); a conversation between Bryce and Newton about ''the transference of energy'' (an oblique sexual reference solidifying their odd double relationship); Mary-Lou urinating in her panties after a dehydrated Newton sheds his earthling disguise; officials demolishing an unexplained space station; a slightly more explicit scene of Newton on an operating table with his pectorals being carved; and a bizarre S&M session in which Newton fires blanks from a revolver at an aging Mary-Lou when she visits him during his confinement.

For three years, Americans are compromised with this eviscerated entry until Cinema 5 (now ALMI) at last releases a complete version just in time for a Roeg retrospective in New York, which coincides with *Bad Timing*'s premiere (1980). But, regardless of resulting mishaps, *The Man Who Fell To Earth* (with *Eureka* following a close second) is Roeg's most beautiful, most tortuous and best realized work—the compendium of all his past and future efforts to alienate and communicate at the same time.

FLASH GORDON and HAMMETT

With David Bowie as a box office maypole, *The Man Who Fell To Earth* leaves Roeg with a career conflict that intensifies in the following years: a vacillation between being a cult director who confounds and a possible Hollywood hopeful who placates. One of Roeg's more imperious temptors is Dino De Laurentiis who approaches him to direct *Flash Gordon*. Roeg is intrigued by Alex Raymond's serial creation and relishes the opportunity. Laurentiis is enthused, yet cautious enough to monitor Roeg's progress during the planning stages.

To facilitate his vision, Roeg enlists the designer Ferdinando Scarfiotti to help create a futuristic landscape which also includes elements of Grand Opera. Roeg explains that he wants a treatment of *Flash* that "concerns love, betrayal and adventure." "By the time Alex Raymond had finished the series, he'd obviously changed his mind about a lot of things. Flash Gordon had become very different, not just a lunking hero, but a thinking person with feelings."

Despite his Herculean effort, Roeg is finally turned down because his version does not meet Laurentiis's mercenary specifications. However, the garrulous Italian still solicits the director's input, but Roeg refuses the offer (probably foreseeing the lackluster Mike Hodges version that Laurentiis later sponsors). So what could have been a unique twist to an old story is left unrealized, except for the Scarfiotti drawings, now destined at best to be an excellent coffee table volume, if an interested publisher can ever get hold of them. Another aborted project during this period is a screen adaptation of Joseph Gores's novel *Hammett* (based on Dashiell Hammett's life and work), which the transplanted German director Wim Wenders later makes with Frederick Forrest. Gores even writes his own screenplay for Roeg, which is also never used in the Wenders version. It is another of those speculations subject to financial, bureaucratic and political quirks, as well as the lack of cooperation from its two prospective stars, Robert Redford and Warren Beatty. There is, however, one positive side to the *Hammett* experience: According to Roeg's Hollywood agent Robert Littman, Joseph Gores is impressed enough by Roeg's insights into the character that he confesses he wishes he had known Roeg even before starting the novel.

BAD TIMING (A Sensual Obsession)

A sick film made by sick people, about sick people, for sick people.

For a movie to get this kind of send-off from its own distributor, it has to have something good going for it. That is exactly the state of affairs when the conservative and quasi-Methodist Rank Organization sees *Bad Timing*'s jagged plunge into the seamy side of "normal" relationships nothing short of highbrow pornography. Rank reacts so strongly that one of its representatives telephones Roeg shortly after the film's release to announce that they are taking their cherished Gong Man emblem off of all British prints.

Anyone deeming *Bad Timing* "not for the squeamish" would be making a feckless understatement. This is a film as vile as it is beautiful; so brutal that it earns Roeg's first official "X" rating since *Performance*. It is the story of a doomed love affair between a research psychiatrist named Alex Linden (Art Garfunkel) and a sybaritic young woman named Milena Flaherty Vodnik (Theresa Russell).

The film's relationship starts off with a few tender moments but soon deteriorates into a mortal battle of personalities. We follow their love as it falters: Milena leaves behind Stefan Vodnik

(Denholm Elliott), a husband old enough to be her father, to join
Alex. As Milena gets more seductive, Alex becomes more and more
obsessed with uncovering her enigmatic past. Alex's curiosity intensifies as he tries to infiltrate and dominate every facet of her life, in-
itiating a series of horrid altercations leading to Milena's suicide attempt. Then, the voyeuristic entanglement acquires one more
player when a detective, Frederich Netusil (Harvey Keitel), enters
the story and conducts an investigation into the events precipitating
the drug overdose. However, by the story's end, we are never certain how much is fact or wish fulfillment, nor can we really tell
whose wishes are being fulfilled.

   Bad Timing (originally to be titled *Illusions*) is based on an Italian
story by Constanzo Constantini called *Ho Tentato Di Vivere*. It is
then transposed into a screenplay by Yale Udoff, a former American
critic and current playwright whose accomplishments include the
Stanley Drama Award-winning *The Club* and the ABC TV movie
Hitchhike. Roeg and Udoff set the story in Vienna—the world's spy
capital as well as Sigmund Freud's birthplace. Concurrently, there
are constant references to espionage, searching, intrusion, betrayal
and identity turmoil. In this respect, *Bad Timing* is really a sequel to
Carol Reed's *The Third Man*—the post-war spy thriller already
glimpsed at in *The Man Who Fell To Earth* and whose famous
theme song Roeg alludes to in a scene where Alex tries to find out
more about Milena through an unidentified third party. *Bad Timing*
tells us how the duplicity and suspicion surrounding the city have
not really altered since World War II. Keitel's part as the sinister
sleuth is quite similar to Trevor Howard's role as Inspector
Calloway, especially with regard to his liaison function between the
male and female leads.

   After *The Man Who Fell To Earth*, Roeg retreats from huge land-
scapes to marinate once again in a claustrophobic setting which
makes Vienna as clammy as the Venice scenes in *"Don't Look
Now"*. From the film's beginning, Roeg lets on that he does not intend to play fair. Alex and Milena already have a dark cloud hanging
over them when Tom Waits's plaintive "Invitation to the Blues"
plays over the credits and the couple examines Gustav Klimt paintings which, like the film, are visually stunning, fragmented and
emotionally cold.

   Bad Timing proves to be a harrowing love story in both reel and real life. As usual, Roeg has difficulty getting the project started. After his two big cancellations and the need to pad his finances by doing television commercials, Roeg manages to get producer Jeremy Thomas's approval only when assuming fifty percent of the responsibility for procuring funds. The Rank Organization is willing to help partly because *Bad Timing* promises to be an educational film that is daring enough to have Freudian overtones at a time when Freud is not all that fashionable.

The actors Roeg initially has in mind for Alex and Milena are Bruno Ganz and Sissy Spacek, but they are already engaged in other projects. For Ganz's replacement, Roeg returns to the unorthodox talents of a pop star with Garfunkel, who is perfect for the role of a Jewish shrink on a crusade in Vienna to live out a Freudian fantasy. This is also the first of the interminable Theresa Russell series, proving to be a watershed for her career since, at only twenty-two years old, she performs a dramatic dare.

Russell, a moody woman with unmistakable California conduct, already catches Roeg's eye five years previously with her small role in Elia Kazan's *The Last Tycoon* and apparently remains stuck in his mind. When he picks her for Milena, Roeg adopts Russell as his most formidable dangerous acquaintance—a relationship which eventually produces two offspring, a marriage and an indelible mark on Roeg's work. *Bad Timing* opens the chronicle of this real-life Freudian smorgasbord. For Russell especially, the attraction is instantaneous as she feels herself "pulled closer and closer" into Roeg's exotic personality. Roeg, on the other hand, probably looks upon Russell's wrinkle-free wiles with the animus and awe of an older gent prostrate beneath the kind of femme fatales to which *Bad Timing* constantly refers.

Regardless of how much Roeg's private life may or may not permeate *Bad Timing*, the film's outcome certainly traumatizes other cast and crew members. Russell and Garfunkel are dumbfounded at Roeg's shooting strategies. He spends much time photographing them from behind and makes them assume sundry immodest postures. Richard Hartley, the film's musical director, admits to Roeg that he would not have been able to work on the project a few years beforehand because he recognizes himself in Alex Linden's gruesome personality. Among the first persons to react strongly to the film's abusive language and sex is another of Rank's minions who, during filming, tells Roeg, ''I'm glad I'm doing it, but I don't want to eat it!''

Once production is almost finished, a pall descends with Garfunkel as its most tragic casualty. From the start, Roeg is intrigued by Garfunkel and studies his every mannerism. Garfunkel, of course, feels the pressure, and has apprehensions the more he and the director interact. In a later *Rolling Stone* interview, he confesses that *Bad Timing* brings him closer to his unconscious than ever before—a shocker to this sometimes mathematics instructor who considers himself a rational thinker. Suddenly he lives out the nightmare of a borderline psychotic: ''I had the picture of myself as if I were a blade, or as if there were a knife in my hand and the arm controlling it was randomly, loosely swinging.'' Ironically, these violent urges overflow on the very day that he is compelled to re-read the Bible's Twenty-third psalm which assures us that ''The Lord is my shepherd, he restores me when I'm in trouble, he takes me into the valley of the shadow of death.''

Immediately after reading the psalm, Garfunkel has a fatal vision of his real fiancée, Laurie Bird. Then, just before returning to the States for three more days of shooting, he discovers she has committed suicide in the same manner as Milena in the film. Distressed by the uncanny connection, Roeg later confesses that *Bad Timing* ''fucked up more people in my crew than anything else I've done. I know five people whose lives were turned over by that movie, including the cameraman, producer and executive producer. I'm kind of glad it got a limited release.''

EUREKA

Eureka is indisputably Roeg's most exhilarating and devastating adventure: his elemental accomplishment and his biggest commercial flop. Here is his unprecedented journey into dementia, picking up where *Bad Timing* leaves off by allowing the protagonist to realize his obsession, and then spend the rest of his life coping with the anticlimax. This is another work serving as companion piece to Roeg's internal bedlam as he, like his main character, knows he could be making his very last visionary stab before submitting to mediocrity.

The film's hero (if we can even use the term) is Jack McCann

(Gene Hackman), who discovers gold in the Yukon after an exhausting search. Under the spiritual auspices of a clairvoyant prostitute named Frieda (Helena Kallioniotes), McCann no sooner stakes his find than he is catapulted twenty years later as an elderly man, nostalgic about his past and wary of his future. He spends these last, tenuous days surrounded by a sycophantic assortment: a melancholic, alcoholic wife, Helen (Jane Lapotaire); a bon vivant playboy for a son-in-law whom he despises named Claude Maillot Van Horn (Rutger Hauer); Charles Perkins (Ed Lauter), a questionable friend and business partner; a crew of suspicious looking house servants; and a ruthless gangster named Mayakovsky (modeled after Meyer Lansky and played by Joe Pesce), who, along with his shady lawyer Aurelio D'Matto (Mickey Rourke), operates a covert deal to appropriate McCann's Luna Bay property and build an illicit gambling casino.

However, *Eureka*'s most significant figure is Tracy (Theresa Russell), Jack's high spirited daughter who, by the end of the film, becomes her father's soul-clone. The story progresses as Jack realizes he is alone against a throng of enemies and misguided companions. His refusal to placate the gangster's wishes culminates in his hideous killing and a subsequent trial in which Tracy must defend husband Claude against the murder charge.

Eureka is loosely based on Marshall Houts's book *King's X*, concerning the actual trial of a prospector named Sir Harry Oakes who, after discovering gold, became one of the world's wealthiest men as well as a friend to the Duke of Windsor. Windsor is at one point part of *Eureka*'s script, but nagging legal problems prevent Roeg and Mayersberg from using him. However, the mystery surrounding Oakes's savage demise remains intact, along with the fact that Oakes's son-in-law, a French count, was the first person accused of the crime and subsequently acquitted.

Perhaps Paul Mayersberg, Roeg's most controversial collaborator (returning after *The Man Who Fell To Earth*), best elucidates the reasons behind *Eureka*'s seemingly uneven and convoluted structure: "The challenge of writing the script was to show convincingly one man's life in two such short, intense bursts . . . It's as if his story began before there were any humans, and ends after all the humans have gone from the world." This explains why the film wanders from realistic drama, to soap opera, to romance, to allegory and even to splatter film at unpredictable intervals. The fact that Houts's book deals mainly with accounts of the Oakes trial is important because *Eureka*'s courtroom scene (in which Tracy takes control of the narrative) is the film's true denouement. This is the moment when Roeg enters his most soul-searching and stylistic quandary, a hallmark performance despite widespread criticisms of its tedium, abstract dialogue and questionable dramatics.

It is, however, inaccurate and unfair to say that the trial scene is *Eureka*'s fifth column. There are strikes against the film which have nothing to do with its content. While elaborate production is underway, no one involved with the project suspects that it will end up being unwanted and unseen. It actually begins as Roeg's anticipated passport out of cultdom and into profit, with Gene Hackman as the cash bait. Getting full support from MGM/UA head David Begelman (who had previously disappointed Roeg with *Out of Africa*), *Eureka* is reportedly Roeg's first double-digit budget film with $10 million put towards thirty months of shooting on location in Canada, Miami, Jamaica and in England's Twickenham Studios. During the Canada sequences, the cast and crew endure the area's worst winter in fifty years, with temperatures of forty degrees below zero, often snowbound in ten foot drifts and forced to retreat to the mountains for days on end.

But the awful weather later proves to be more clement than the insecure and irresponsible climate at MGM/UA, which undergoes severe personnel revamping. Begelman—the film's main benefactor—is forced to resign after a financial scandal, and, as a result, *Eureka* falls victim to internecine studio squabbles. The film barely survives through four successive studio bosses, including one who has absolutely no regard for either the film or its distribution possibilities. It is instead dumped onto the lap of UA Classics, which never officially releases it to the general American public until hitting the video market in 1985. Its few press screenings are mostly unfavorable. It plays in England for a limited run, but in America, after two years of neglect, is released to several art houses in the bigger cities to get equally dismal responses. *San Francisco Chronicle* critic Judy Stone allegedly storms out of the theater screaming that "It's the biggest bunch of horseshit I've ever seen." But *Film Comment*'s Harlan Kennedy calls *Eureka* "a treasure-trail of optic clues, mythic psychedelia and eyeblink rags of illusion and allusion, which lead into one of the richest movie labyrinths since *Citizen Kane*.

Apart from all of the hoopla that it is Roeg's most muddled contribution, *Eureka* is, in many respects, surprisingly accessible. Much of it even has the look of a television mini-series with similar family and monetary intrigues. The imagery also has its source in tangible folklore and legend. Whereas *The Man Who Fell To Earth* is riddled with metaphors without a recognizable mythology, *Eureka* draws generously from Kabbalah, alchemy and semi-historical Germanic tales. Perhaps the biggest gripe some of the tonier critics raise is that the film flirts too much with cliché while pretending to be too original. *Variety* moans because ''Most of the film's characters are basically familiar to the point of corny, and with most it's just hard to give a damn.'' But such responses lend the film an even greater aura of mystery. Most who are familiar with Roeg's best work realize that he does not delve into cliché without a deeper purpose in mind.

The one quality about *Eureka* that is both problematic and fascinating is the manner in which it assaults the audience with contrary perspectives, embroiled in its own race war between McCann's Wagnerian quest and his enemy Mayakovsky's Semitic world view that mixes Old Testament retribution with Freudianism. The film begins as a Faustian adventure as McCann strives for earthly power at the risk of losing his soul. For him, gold is more than an acquisition. It embodies a supernatural wisdom that guides him even before he makes the discovery. Once the mysterious stone falls into his hands to save him from a pack of hungry wolves, he unwittingly makes a pact with entities that render his triumph and harbor his downfall. Like Albrecht in Wagner's *Ring*, McCann forsakes love to attain his divine alloy. Also, as Frieda predicts his success and laments over their failed romance, she acts as Faust's Gretchen, acknowledging that her love has no place in the hero's demonic mission. We flash ahead to McCann in late middle age, at home among his spoils, bored yet apprehensive. Then, in comes his wife Helen who, like Faust's Helena, is a domesticating influence helping to channel McCann's overweening energies into business and connubial matters. Mayersberg also writes the script with thoughts of Goethe's novel *Elective Affinities*, which portrays its character relations less from psychological and more from innate chemical interactions. *Eureka* as well tries to make its characters into larger-than-life prototypes fulfilling some cyclic edda, whose origins are largely Nordic.

The closer McCann gets to death, the more Mayakovsky's venal belief system supplants the Teutonic excesses. First seen in his synagogue, the gangster thinks his God provides him with a strange justification for any greedy ambition. In one instance, when Mayakovsky contemplates McCann's murder, two elderly rabbis stare back at him from a photograph while he ridicules McCann for having no faith in a world where "there is only one God among us schmucks." While plotting to appropriate a portion of Luna Bay, he believes he can get McCann's approval through psychological manipulation, at one point paraphrasing Freud as his modern-day Moses by declaring "If you understand a man's desires, you understand the man." The gangster's Hebrew ghosts also resurface through Claude, who shares an equal interest in the Kabbalah and combs through a Tree-of-Life numerical chart to predict the next time McCann falls ill.

Especially once *Eureka* concentrates on the dynamics of the four principals—McCann, Helen, Tracy and Claude—any attempt to avoid psychologizing, especially with Freudian and Rankian references, fails. The film turns into a family romance with the Oedipal struggle reversed: the father and daughter unite against the mother and son-in-law. Even *Eureka*'s main publicity photo has psychosexual overtones as it depicts Tracy and McCann looking more like the bride and groom while Claude and Helen observe covetously from the sidelines.

Roeg's attempt to meld ideologies and myths backfires when he is confronted with charges of anti-Semitism, even though he is the only person on the crew to wear a yarmulke while shooting the sequence with Mayakovsky in the same synagogue that Meyer Lansky helped to restore. The film's religious amalgam also gets more intense with the mad voodoo sequence which Claude attends the night Jack is murdered. The elaborately staged dances, chants, chicken mutilations and amatory gyrations seem very authentic, due to the fact that Roeg employs several Haitian magicians to assist him.

Eureka overflows into narrative bedlam because Roeg allows his obsessions to take control more than ever before. As in the past, he is best when his passion grapples with form; and this film will be remembered as the work by which his future efforts must be measured.

Strangely enough, critics tend not to object to *Eureka*'s cycloramic camera or disconcerting edits so much as the dramatic dialogue which seems overly poetic. Reacting to the highly verbal trial scene, one *Variety* critic complains:

> With striking lack of self-confidence, the film concluded with a gratuitous piece of voice-overed philosophy to the effect that the excitement comes from the quest rather than the achievement. If an audience has to be told, what's the point of the preceding two hours-plus of tortured, convoluted narrative?

Roeg indeed seems fully aware that the obtrusive dialogue undercuts his visual power. With *Fahrenheit 451* and *Performance*, he displays an interest in the verbal-visual paradox, but *Eureka* takes it over the top. The film's words stick in people's minds more than the images. This is also the first time in twelve years that Roeg changes photographers, letting Alex Thompson's harsher contrasts replace Anthony Richmond's more dreamy look—the end result being a visual style that, at times, looks more conventional (especially in the interior scenes) but remains chilling. It is also important to note that *Eureka* intensifies an ongoing controversy about Roeg. Those who credit him only for his visual wonders miss the point. Roeg is most fascinating when he embodies the struggle between cinematic and literary sensibilities. His films imply that, no matter how ornate and visually hypnotic the story gets, there is always something missing until words complete the picture.

This is also the first time Roeg employs Stanley Myers to direct the music. Myers manages to supply beautiful and eerie atonal themes mixed with syrupy soundtracks to make the film go from being overly sentimental to ice cold. Critics and audiences may find *Eureka* "perverse" because of the manner in which it refuses to stay confined to one mood—an effect enhanced by Myers's ability to displace the atmospherics at just the right time.

Eureka could very well be Roeg's career fluke, a fit of genius that will not and cannot be repeated, a last surge of pure mania "followed by decades of despair" when mid-1980s conservative demands reduce most movies to extended television commercials. At this time, cinema reverts to its tawdry beginnings as a peep show nurtured on nepotism and programmed to churn out linear pabulum. With the advent of rock video and the hyper-sophistication of television ads, film proper at last takes second place.

Roeg is among few directors at this time to confirm the scary suspicion that film, like literature, drama and painting, has become another moribund art form that can only validate its aesthetic by flaunting its unique failure. So, *Eureka* can be seen as a negentropic exercise to contort film's outmoded parameters into an altogether new and more beautiful monster that defies description. Perhaps *Eureka*'s talkiness is Roeg's attempt to escape from visual culture's tyranny, much like the "textualist" experiments of postmodern theater which give words a pre-eminence that past demands on performer presence had denied. *Eureka*'s dialogue may, in fact, appear as awkward and extraneous today as his visual style did twenty years before.

INSIGNIFICANCE, CASTAWAY and TELEVISION ART

Just before *Insignificance*'s release, Roeg directs a few rock videos of his own with people like Pink Floyd's Roger Waters ("The Pros and Cons of Hitchhiking") and Tom Robinson. But he, like such directors as Martin Scorsese and Ridley Scott, plays an even more interesting role in directing arty television commercials. Indeed, ad agencies put Roeg through almost as many obstacles as movie studios. After doing ads for J&B Scotch Whiskey, Roeg works through James Garrett & Sons for Coca-Cola and finds himself amidst one of the biggest hush campaigns in market history. Apparently, everyone involved with the commercial is kept in the dark about what they are doing and learn only afterward that Coke is trying to conceal their new, and later failed, plan to impose a new taste formula on its public. Roeg also runs into frustration with his ad for the up and coming British Telecom. The commercial takes four days to make, with over one hundred extras at a budget of £100,000. But when completed, Telecom feels it is too good and fears that its market share will be over-stimulated. The ad is never used since Telecom decides on something "less dramatic."

The pressures involved in compressing a mood or idea into thirty to sixty seconds are particularly challenging for Roeg who, up till now, is known for his indifference to pacing consistency. In the process, he manages to produce some interesting pieces, an example of which is an ad for Terry's Moonlight Chocolates. The commercial involves a rooftop, candlelit dinner with the motif of a woman's red dress contrasting against a black background. Another visually arresting ad, which also raises predictable controversy, is a Government-sponsored service announcement for AIDS prevention. Here, he is in keeping with his reputation for off-base, if not overwrought, symbolism as an exploding volcano connotes the contraband orgasm. One critic from London's *The Independent* is incredulous:

> Why is everyone being so secretive about the identity of the director who made the Government's television commercial about AIDS? . . . Perhaps someone decided that the New Celibacy might not be helped by association with Roeg's name. *Bad Timing*'s main claim to fame is the scene where Art Garfunkel has a nasty attack of necrophilia, in glorious technicolour, on Theresa Russell's naked and lifeless body. It gives a whole new layer of meaning to the gravestone in the AIDS commercial.

Working for the eighties television market has a lasting impact on Roeg's style. *Insignificance* and *Castaway* have the properties of glossy advertisements. Their comparatively tight and cohesive structures may thrill larger audiences but disappoint many hardcore devotees addicted to his weirdness. It is obvious that *Eureka* scares Roeg into thinking twice about rubbing too hard against commercial considerations. So, in some respects, these subsequent two films can be interpreted as both a means of atonement as well as an experiment to see how well he can encompass his complex ideas into simpler formats.

Insignificance reveals a director who, at least temporarily, stops shouting in the dark and massages his audience with designer forceps. Being what *Variety* calls "Roeg's most accessible film since *Walkabout*," *Insignificance* seems less dense and more flat than his previous work. But the style suits the content. The film is about public images and those unable to escape them. It is set on a sweltering August evening in New York City in 1954. Four of America's most influential media figures miraculously cross paths.

Attempting to promote her latest picture, The Actress (Theresa Russell parodying Marilyn Monroe) stands before a phalanx of movie cameras as a windy subway grate blows her dress open. The Professor (Michael Emil resembling Albert Einstein) sits in his hotel room unaware that The Actress will soon pay him a visit just after he is hounded by The Senator (Tony Curtis as Joe McCarthy) who tries to pressure him into testifying before the HUAC panel. When The Actress escapes from the salivating crowd to impress The Professor with her interpretation of the Theory of Relativity, her jealous husband, The Ballplayer (Gary Busey as a variation on Joe DiMaggio), enters to start a domestic feud that will not terminate until The Professor describes for The Actress the shape of the physical universe. But his hasty summary cannot abate a marriage nurtured on infidelities and failed pregnancies; so he leaves the room for the couple to mend their problems.

Then, the next morning, after The Ballplayer exits, The Senator returns with his thugs, inflamed by his impotent performance the previous night with a prostitute made up to look like The Actress. In the process of serving The Professor with a House subpoena, he finds The Actress emerging from beneath the bed covers. He nervously scurries about the room collecting The Professor's calculus for court evidence while The Actress tries to save the work by bartering her sexual favors. Inveigling her into accepting the offer, he pummels her in the gut and attempts to run off with the papers before The Professor returns to stop him. This time, The Professor responds to the threats by throwing his life's work out the window just as the wounded Actress miscarriages again. When her husband returns, she sends him off with a declaration that their marriage is over. She is alone again with The Professor, but before leaving, insists that he reveal his private thoughts which have all along been roving back to the fateful hour of 8:15 when the Enola Gay sprayed its spleen over Hiroshima. The Professor refuses to assuage his guilt for inspiring the bomb and, when The Actress prepares to exit, we enter his point of view as he envisions her destroyed by a nuclear conflagration.

Roeg gets the idea to film *Insignificance* through another of his synchronicities. Never an avid theater-goer, he decides to see Terry Johnson's play with some friends, including the wife of his producer

Jeremy Thomas. A few weeks afterward, the idea hits him: "An incident came up in my own life, and I thought, good God, nobody knows a damn thing about anyone. That was the very first premise that started me thinking about the piece again. They didn't know anything about each other, The Actress, The Ballplayer . . . Famous people are only perceived images; they're inventions, everything's an invention . . ." Roeg compares this film to some of playwright Joe Orton's mordant, absurdist farces which poke fun at the western world's most sacred cows. *Insignificance*'s lasting image epitomizes America's sex-death obsession: the metaphor of Marilyn Monroes's flowing dress and Hiroshima's mushroom cloud.

When Roeg retains Johnson to adapt this stage drama into a screenplay, the result is a concentration of material with many scenes excised. Johnson has to help edit over two hours of drama into a neater 110 minutes. All the while, Roeg, as usual, pays full respect to the screenwriter and lets him have as much freedom as is necessary, only adding suggestions to make it consistent with the look of a screwball comedy.

What the film achieves, which for obvious reasons the play cannot, is a graphic rendering of a nuclear holocaust which flashes in and out of the story. Johnson credits the chief inspiration for those moments to a book called *The Impossible Fire*, which consists of drawings by Hiroshima and Nagasaki survivors. Roeg and Johnson also intend to have more references, such as a scene (of which we see a trace) of a hotel room loaded with Japanese peace delegates arguing about the bomb. Roeg also wants the narrative to run (in a similar manner to *The Man Who Fell To Earth*) with a train motif as the time link, mostly through The Professor's perspective as he looks out of a train window when as a child and as an adult. But production timing and budget-tightening kill the idea. The film's major publicity gimmick, however, is retained and produced on schedule: a portrait of The Actress by David Hockney, consisting of a semi-Cubist mosaic of polaroids superimposed on each other to form her sprawled, naked body.

Christening Roeg's acceptance into larger circles, *Insignificance* opens the 1985 Cannes Film Festival, an event made slightly sour by Alexander Walker's off-color snipe about it being the only British entry made in America about Americans with all American actors.

At this time, even Roeg's public persona changes. No longer the
withdrawn chimera answering questions with a studied vagueness,
he seems a calmer man, talking more about love's dynamics with
humanistic candor while resting on his thorny laurels.

Everybody has their secret lives, where even secrets have secrets.
                                    —Gerald Kingsland in *Castaway*

With the release of his eighth feature, *Castaway*, Roeg provides us
with a hybrid of *Walkabout* and *Bad Timing*—an impossible relationship far away from civilization which becomes a battle for
spiritual and physical survival. It is based on an autobiographical account of the same name by Lucy Irvine (Amanda Donohoe), relating
her ordeal after she answers a newspaper ad for a one-year romance
with a certain Gerald Kingsland (Oliver Reed) on a deserted tropical
island.

Castaway is a variation on a previous unfilmed Roeg project about
the failed journey of Donald Crowhurst, a British eccentric who had
attempted to sail around the world by himself against international
competition. Though his trip was faltering miserably, Crowhurst
managed to radio optimistic progress reports and keep a fake
logbook. What interests Roeg most is the Crowhurst diary later
found which contains the incoherent ranting of a man gone mad at
sea.

Another of Roeg's sources is Defoe's *Robinson Crusoe* and the
controversies regarding the author's documentary accuracy in
relating Alexander Selkirk's adventures. Occult dabbler Colin
Wilson expresses similar educated doubts about Defoe's
verisimilitude in his book *A Criminal History of Mankind*, which
strangely is among the reading matter Lucy finds in Gerald's posses-
sion just when their venture is almost over.

When Roeg and screenwriter Allan Scott team up again after
"Don't Look Now" to interpret Irvine's reports, they have doubts
about her veracity from the start. The film remains quite faithful to
her accounts, even to the details of the marriage she and Kingsland
must undergo in order for Australian authorities to grant them permission to inhabit the island of Tuin (located at the country's
northernmost tip). Then again, we cannot help but detect that Roeg
is again tricking us. *Castaway* seems Roeg's most simplistic and ac-

cessible narrative to date, but he actually concentrates all of his usual thematic layers and cherished ambiguities into the Irvine character. He transforms her from an omniscient narrator into an enigma. As the film progresses, we must constantly ask ourselves: What are her true motives for undertaking the journey? Why does she suffer through all of the romantic preliminaries (dinner dates, perfunctory seductions) and even reluctantly marry the man, only to refuse his advances once they arrive on Tuin? Why does she stay faithful to the marriage contract even though she does not really love Gerald and will probably never see him again when their year's trial is over? Are darker motives involved?

The same audience that might be taken in by *Castaway*'s simplicity may actually find the Irvine character's inconsistencies as annoying as *The Man Who Fell To Earth*'s time discrepancies. But, as we watch Lucy recoil from Gerald and draw herself closer to her inanimate surroundings, we resign ourselves to confusion over her proclivities. This is the film's true conflict: the hook that keeps us guessing.

In his previous attempts at exploring the female viewpoint, Roeg often presents a woman dissatisfied with imposed social and sexual norms. Certainly, Roeg even identifies somewhat with the Irvine figure, but his intentions get more puzzling because of the disproportionate amount of time he spends penetrating Gerald's psyche, drawing more attention to Lucy through systematic neglect. This is partly because the real Irvine is equally intriguing. Her book is an adjunct to another called *Runaway*, which attempts to explicate her motivations for writing the first book. Irvine's other autobiographical accounts include being raped at an early age, being plagued with an intense identity crisis, and a final cataclysmic rise to stardom allowing her to quit a low paying clerical job and ensconce under the label "multimillionaire" (with a newly-registered I.Q. of 188).

While Irvine's writing chronicles her feelings *ad nauseam*, Roeg prefers to make her into another of his mysterious matriarchs. It is never made clear whether the prospect of writing a book about the excursion is the sole motive, especially since she lacks Gerald's lustful enthusiasm. On their first dinner date, Lucy already expresses distaste for Gerald's corny machismo by hinting that she has no intention of becoming his "Man Friday," despite his insistence

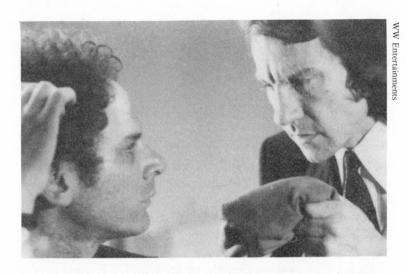

THE OTHER LOVE STORY
HARVEY KEITEL CONFESSES TO ART GAFUNKEL IN *BAD TIMING*

THE PROFESSOR (MICHAEL EMIL) MEETS
THE ACTRESS (THERESA RUSSELL) IN *INSIGNIFICANCE*

FAMILY ROMANCE FROM *EUREKA*
l. to r.: JANE LAPOTAIRE, GENE HACKMAN, THERESA
RUSSELL, RUTGER HAUER

on having "a woman who can cook, sew, fish and put up a tent."

Castaway may start out with the now classic seventies scenario of two middle-class malcontents embarking on a hedonistic caprice. But once the illusions die and sex is no longer possible, we get a painful lesson in what happens to relationships when only the amenities remain and lovers must settle for being mutual nursemaids. Beset by infectious lesions, malnutrition and weakened spirits, they gaze at the stars one night while Lucy reminds Gerald that "This may be the place where we die"—apprehensions which almost come true later when they are near death and two nuns (Georgina Hale and Frances Barber) arrive just in time to save them.

Roeg refers to *Castaway* as his first "post-AIDS film." It assumes a whole new meaning when we consider AIDS as its oblique metaphor. For this reason, Roeg is perhaps being sardonic by presenting it in the guise of heterosexual slapstick: vignettes of nuptial nerdiness vacillating between an apotheosis and a parody on the missionary position.

The story is most salient in the first part when Lucy and Gerald are still gripped by their civilization. Similar to *Walkabout* (which begins in Sydney before moving to the outback), *Castaway* reveals an urban morass that is no more claustrophobic than the "natural" world. London (which Roeg has not filmed since *Performance*) is damp and gray during morning rush hour as Lucy goes to her dreary desk job at the British Inland Revenue; while Gerald, a schoolteacher, prepares himself for a semi-aquatic existence by giving swimming instructions to his pupils. Roeg externalizes Lucy's foreboding by filling the moments leading up to her "ultimate blind date" with news reports of homicides, kidnappings, rapes, as well as the Pope's assassination attempt and a facetious clip about the Royal Wedding between Prince Charles and Di.

Castaway does remind us of *The Man Who Fell To Earth* when Roeg allows a movie on television to act as a chorus for the film's situation. Jack Clayton's *The Pumpkin Eater* (about a marriage gone bankrupt) appears on both Gerald's and Lucy's tubes the night they arrange to meet. From the moment they come face to face in a Russell Square hotel lobby, Clayton's film seems to orchestrate their identity misconceptions and communication tangles. On their first encounter, Gerald even mistakes his date for an older and portlier woman who lurks in the background just before Lucy introduces herself.

The one fascinating Roeg trait retained in this film is the curious treatment of peripheral characters and the practice of crowding portentous associations into very short scenes that end before we can fully assimilate all we are teased into investigating. We see Gerald at home with his two prepubescent sons (Paul Reynolds and Sean Hamilton) who discuss women with a puerile callousness that may actually reveal more about their father's attitudes. There is also Lucy's homely and seemingly sexless roommate Lara (Sorrell Johnson), who is politely disaffected by Gerald's vulgarity. The sinister publisher (Joseph Blatchley) holds Lucy to her book agreement as if it were the nuptial contract she dreads signing.

Among the film's most haunting scenes is the actual wedding, conducted in a tepid atmosphere replete with Muzak, glacial social exchanges and the sound of a prison door slamming before a cut to Lucy crying on her bridal bed. Later, on the island, when enough time elapses for their bodies and minds to deteriorate, Lucy and Gerald are visited by two attractive Australian lifeguards, Jason (Tony Rickards) and Rod (Todd Rippon), who come to deliver a census. Gerald's fears of being a cuckold are intensified when Lucy is almost seduced by one of them before she resists with the flimsy excuse of being "a married woman."

Until this film, Roeg's style retains a cult following largely because of the way he addresses the angst and weary "decadence" of post-sixties youth. But now, with *Castaway*'s more accessible narrative and allusion to the eighties season of pestilence, this relationship seems to, at least for the time being, draw to a close. Although he personally loves the film, producer Rick McCallum admits that this is one that the director makes as an act of conscience to explore his private feelings about relationships in a manner to which larger audiences may relate. *Castaway* also brings Roeg a record number of praiseworthy letters, the vast majority written by female viewers impressed by his sensitivity.

During the pre-production phase, Roeg and Scott decide on an untimely rewrite after going out of their way to finalize the script in Los Angeles. When shooting commences, Amanda Donohoe's boyfriend continuously upsets the sessions by taking it upon himself to give her acting lessons during takes. Roeg also hires a sleight-of-hand artist to teach Oliver Reed several tricks displayed in the film.

Reed, reportedly in another of his drunken and pugilistic moods, invites the magician to his home and proceeds to chase him around his
yard with mock threatening gestures.

Castaway also has a few production problems. Roeg and his
associates decide not to shoot the film on Tuin and choose the
Seychelles for varying reasons. According to Allan Scott, Tuin's
ninety-eight percent humidity factor makes shooting impossible.
But Rick McCallum gives a more penurious reason: simply that the
direct flights available from London are hard to pass up. Even the
Seychelles present weather problems. At times, the temperature is
so high that, according to cinematographer Harvey Harrison,
camera electronics have to be packed in a silica gel. The natural
sunlight is too excessive to allow any scenic texture; so they are
forced to employ artificial light. During some close-ups between the
actors, black sheets are used to keep out sunlight altogether. Many
of the daytime scenes are actually shot at night.

The Seychelles offer another advantage: massive rock formations
resembling the human anatomy. This allows the story's animism
—Lucy's love affair with the island—to appear as a constant graphic
reminder. At times, *Castaway* is visual Muzak that seems to borrow
heavily from Club Med advertisements. Roeg uses photographer
Joel Meyrowitz's *Cape Light* as part of his inspiration. For the
various underwater scenes, which are not planned in the script but
materialize as shooting commences, Roeg uses Mike Valentine,
known for his marine photography in the film *The Deep*.

Castaway, like *Eureka*, is also victim to management buyouts. It
begins as a UBA (United British Artists) property, but Virgin pulls
out of the project for financial reasons. Four weeks go into shooting
before Thorn-EMI, which takes over sponsorship, comes close to
bankruptcy. So, Cannon arrives to the rescue—an intervention more
absurd than divine since no two people are more at odds with Roeg's
vision than Golan and Globus, who are Hollywood's answer to
Procter and Gamble as procurers of the mundane. Part of the
American distribution delay results from debates over how the film
will be marketed. When the production is finished and proves to be
popular in Britain (following its premiere at the 1987 London Film
Festival), Cannon wants to exploit Donohoe's nudity and sell
Castaway in America as another of their beachbum tit flicks. Getting
only piecemeal distribution on the West Coast and parts of the

Midwest, it is not available to most Americans until the video release a year later.

After *Castaway* is shown at the London premiere, Ken Russell (also on hand to debut his masterpiece *Gothic*) credits Roeg's film for being the one movie that every director should make because its geographical limits and universal topic present the ultimate film-making challenges and snags.

Rebounding on TRACK 29

While *Castaway* takes us through connubial follies, Roeg's next projects deliver us again into more unorthodox, and consequently more realistic, sex.

Aria is a special film which boasts of breaking ground but is really an exercise in male menopause. It combines ten major directors (including Ken Russell, Jean-Luc Godard, Derek Jarman and Julien Temple) and their psychosexual interpretations of various operas. Roeg fashions a bizarre slant to Giuseppe Verdi's *The Masked Ball*. Theresa Russell is cast this time as a woman who looks out onto a Vienna landscape and imagines that she is King Zog, the renowned Monarch of Albania who, after attending Verdi's opera, manages to kill a would-be assassin. Roeg calls this story, partly taken from historical fact, *King Zog Shot Back*. Here, Roeg alters history to its better advantage. The opera Zog actually attended on his assassination night was *Il Pagliacci*, but Roeg decided *The Masked Ball* was more appropriate. Besides being inspired by King Gustave III of Sweden's assassination, Verdi's *Ball* also made its 1858 premiere the night Napoleon III escaped a murder attempt. Filmed on location in Vienna in just two and one-half days on a budget of £15,000, this fifteen minute vignette has characteristic Roeg touches: a close-up of a knife against an opera performer's bare breasts juxtaposed with blood dripping over an immaculate snowbank. However, the excessive soft focus and sterile period sets make the film look more Zeffirelli than Roeg. Despite this, Roeg manages to capture the look of an early silent film, spicing it up with genderfuck. Theresa Russell with a mustache must be seen to be believed.

The *King Zog* sequence is essentially a family endeavor. Roeg uses his sons as assistants: Waldo Roeg, the eldest, is first assistant director; Nico is unit stills photographer; Luc (now head of his own

media company) is associate producer and Sholto acts as production
runner. Also little Max, at age eighteen months, plays the Baroness'
son.

I personally get to witness Roeg in action at De Lane Lea Studios,
giving *King Zog* some last minute edits. Manned in front of his
Steenbeck, he actually *becomes* the movie, using his thumb and
forefinger as a makeshift gun to act out the shooting while
frantically keeping rhythm to Verdi's score with the other hand.
Also on board is the editor for Roeg's last four films, Tony
Lawson—a shy but amiable man who seems extremely overworked
and a bit frustrated as Roeg asks him to run the assassination scene
several times until the sound and image are properly synchronized.
Lawson, a well-respected film technician who has also worked with
such cranks as Stanley Kubrick, exemplifies the mathematical for-
titude a craftsman needs to counterbalance the mercurial artist
breathing down his neck.

At the time, Roeg is jubilant about his next task *Track 29*, produced through DEG Studios. This story abandons the insipid world
of adult trysts in order to explore the more rewarding treasures of
childhood ''polymorphous perversity.'' The script comes from
Dennis Potter, whom Rick McCallum (also this film's producer)
hails as ''the father of weird British television,'' with such forays as
Pennies From Heaven to his credit.

The most important Potter opus, though, is *The Singing Detective*, a six-part BBC mini-series which vindicates the art of ambiguity
to heights that are foreign to most American couch potatoes. The
protagonist is a detective story writer named Philip Marlow (without
the ''e'') who suffers from extreme psoriasis and is forced to enter a
semi-hallucinatory retrospective of his life while confined to an
infirmary bed. As in *The Man Who Fell To Earth*, this tale uses
nostalgia (mostly through popular songs from a bygone era) in an attempt to conjure some connection between private emotions and our
slippery perspective on history.

The Singing Detective shares several of Roeg's strains: the fond-
ness for trains, parallel editing and identity mergers. It even
outrightly borrows an image from *Bad Timing* when Marlow's
flashbacks of his mother having sex are juxtaposed with doctors
pumping adrenalin into a geriatric patient.

Knowing Potter's excesses, we can only quake and swoon at the unholy concoction that he and Roeg plan. *Track 29* may actually be Roeg's craziest work to date—a possible proof that he has not gone soft.

Its story involves a woman named Linda (Theresa Russell, again) who is disenchanted with her puerile husband and unconsciously lures Martin (Gary Oldman), a young man her exact age who claims to be her illegitimate son. From there, the narrative fluctuates from incestuous intrigue to psychosis since we never know whether or not Martin's visit and subsequent seduction are really happening or just delusions seeping through Linda's repressed memory.

Linda's husband Henry (Christopher Lloyd), when not preoccupied with his toy train set, works as a physician in a geriatric ward. He enjoys an illicit affair with Nurse Stein (Sandra Bernhard), who must periodically don a pair of red surgical gloves, strap him to an examining table and spank his upraised buttocks whenever he misbehaves. And, of course, as in *Bad Timing*, Roeg pulls no Freudian punches. The recurring train theme retains all of its phallic splendor, along with a capricious supply of vaginal allusions (not to mention other orifices). There are numerous Daliesque interludes of human bodies merging with objects: the shape of an earth mound blending into Linda's reclining figure, two colliding trains smashing into a doll's head, and so on.

While shooting on location in Wilmington, North Carolina, Roeg's cranium erupts into a phantasmagoria. In one of the scenes where Linda dreams of being raped in an amusement park, Roeg decides to add (without prior warning) an odd touch. He instructs his crew to set up an enormous boulder to crash through the roof of Linda's house and land on her bed. Fortunately, they come across a Hollywood replica of such a boulder (originally designed for use in Dino De Laurentiis's *King Kong Lives*). Undaunted by this first stunt, Roeg later insists that, in order to amplify the film's sexual metaphor, a truck must crash through a wall. This sends the crew into another dither subsequently eased with persistence and luck.

Track 29 certainly has shades of *The Man Who Fell To Earth* not only with its constant trains but with Martin as an Englishman stranded in an isolated American town. This is also another of Roeg's sardonic commentaries on American life and its baleful influence on the remaining western world's mores. Midpoint in the

story, when Martin thinks he has finally convinced Linda that she is
his "Mummy," he tells her: "I am *entitled* to an American
childhood. Spoiled, pampered, overfed, over-indulged, under-
educated. Everything."

Roeg calls this work his tribute to "immaturity," which he contends is the unavoidable nemesis of any relationship. After
culminating in Henry's gory murder (which Martin previously
enacts through sympathetic magic by destroying the train set),
Track 29 actually surpasses *Bad Timing* in revealing the criminal
outcome of being trapped in other people's opinions of us. This (in
conjunction with his previous two works) shows a tendency to avoid
cluttered subplots and focus more on strained character interactions.
The results of this new direction may either show Roeg at his least
demanding or most terrifying.

THE CAMERA THAT EATS ITSELF

Interview with Paul Mayersberg

The actor now begins to surround the camera.
The camera can no longer cover the action.
The camera has lost the battle with reality.
Art has lost out to life . . .

We continue the movement from trains and planes as well as
cars, an exciting journey through the cities of the world . . .

Images dissolve into and are superimposed on one another
so we begin to get a picture of the world as a city and the city
as a world . . .

THESE LINES FROM AN ABORTED ROEG-MAYERSBERG
project called *Miraclejack* best exemplify the self-referential approach to storytelling that Roeg ultimately prefers and which
Mayersberg encourages. *Miraclejack* ironically triumphs as the consummate screenplay because it is the world's most unfilmable one,
involving physical feats and battles between fantasy and "reality"
which are impossible to contain within any known form.
  Coming close to *Miraclejack* are *The Man Who Fell To Earth* and

Eureka: two Mayersberg scripts which are undoubtedly Roeg's best and most challenging works. Both films wrench themselves away from most strangleholds of convention. They play different genres against each other and contort their stories to elicit contradictory premises, taunting viewers until they must step into the picture to impose their own meanings.

Mayersberg's other filmed scripts include a Canadian spy thriller called *The Disappearance*, with Donald Sutherland; and Nagisa Oshima's controversial *Merry Christmas, Mr. Lawrence*, with David Bowie and Tom Conti. He has also made his first directing effort entitled *Captive*, which explores the psychic power games between a wealthy man (Oliver Reed), his daughter and the daughter's kidnappers.

* * *

Let's start with your comment about America being the last home of the action story.

Yes. American films have an end and work on the principle of the end. You could also say this for Soviet works. It may have to do with the relatively primitive view of things. Stories that don't appear to head towards an end are inherently uninvolving. That's their attitude towards society as much as art. A lot of Soviet writing in particular implies that if there is no end or clear purpose, there is something wrong with it. Russia and America are very similar in that way. While European films work on the principle of the journey and the discovery, America is bound by the genre; and so its cinema has been very much a slave to patents, formal patents of storytelling which can be very interesting because when you have that, then you notice very quickly when somebody breaks that patent. Also, when you have an end in view, you tend to tailor what happens in order to arrive at the end, which gives you a strangely distorted view of people's behavior.

That is why crime novels and thrillers *aren't* literature, because of their attitudes towards motive. Motive has to determine everything, the patent of events based on the motive and the working out of the crime. That is why in most crime stories, you get fairly cardboard characters. Dostoevsky wrote primarily crime stories, and there is certainly no patent of that kind. The storytelling idea is a primitive one, and cinema is dogged by storytelling. I don't think it's a good storytelling medium, personally.

More of a dream medium?

I use the word *irreal*. It's not an English word, it's a French word. It is somewhere between dream-like and anything else you'd care to call it. I don't like classifications. That's why I'm glad that *The Man Who Fell To Earth*, the first film I wrote which got made, is very hard to classify. It's not really science-fiction.

That may explain your interest in the feminine point of view. You rebel against that pioneering spirit that always relies on action instead of contemplation.

Yes. People are very critical if you deviate from this path you are supposed to set yourself on. It probably begins at school.

Towards the end of The Man Who Fell To Earth, *the story frays even more just at the point when you expect it all to tie together. There are details that the Tevis book explains which you obscure.*

The book is very good. We just did a slightly different thing with it. We omitted the political aspect. As far as we were concerned, it was not a story, but an adventure. Adventure doesn't have a form. It can go anywhere. Elizabethan tales or trapper's tales, even something like *Papillon*, do not really have endings, except sometimes when the guy comes home. They seem to be the reverse of tragic forms. In adventure, nothing is pre-determined. Comedy is not the opposite of tragedy, adventure is.

You like dealing with people who lose sight of their goals and get confused. Eureka *takes an American folklore figure like a gold prospector and shows his life when the adventure is over.*
Well, *Eureka* has a special formal problem, which was that the time slip between the beginning and the end is enormous, a sudden gap of twenty years. It is a story of a man who achieved what he set out to do at a sort of awkward point in his life, at around forty. And while the struggle seemed to pay off, because he got what he wanted, then what? In life, it seems to me, stories don't have a given order. The climax has happened in the beginning, not the end. So, we were very interested in the idea of a climax that appeared at a point other than at the end of the story. If you'll notice in *Eureka*, even for the other

characters, the best moments of their lives, the most ecstatic or dramatic moments, tend to occur off-screen or *before* we see them, or even afterwards maybe. We deal with the awkward areas of life, which is most of our lives, because for ninety percent of your life, nothing happens. But they are not less interesting because of that. In fact, they could be very evocative. It's the awkwardness of a story and life that *Eureka* was, in a formal sense, about. Also, he really didn't find the gold, it found him. A clairvoyant had led him to it. It is not the same as the conventional view of someone going out and finding something. He actually did very little to find the gold, except suffer.

How do you feel about Eureka*'s trial scene now?*

Oh, I think the trial scene is a terrifically important part of the film. It is a thing we spent a lot of time on. There are people who do not like the trial scene and feel that it is some kind of terrible mistake. We wanted the trial to expose the characters, how Jack McCann's death affected them all. Instead of saying, "But now he's dead, it's over!," on the contrary, it has only just begun. Like Caesar, who dies at the end of Act II and then you think, "Well, what's the story now? It's over, our hero's dead." But of course it isn't. And then you realize that wasn't the tale at all. *Eureka* has a lot of Shakespearean references, not in order to elevate it into great art, but because in the construction of many of Shakespeare's plays, we find an extremely recondite style. *Macbeth*, of course, uses the idea of the prophecy, and living under the prophecy no matter what.

Lady Macbeth is an extension of her husband, his conscience.

Yes, the character of Lady Macbeth has been much discussed. Her husband is paying the price for not understanding.

Tracy McCann is also Jack's conscience.

And an extension of him. She will become what he was, in another way.

The trial scene's dialogue is like an abstract poem, or a chorus. It is not meant to be taken literally as a drama between two people.

I find that when you extract from a trial the best bits, as you sometimes do when you are reporting it, you get lines like that. So,

what I did was write a scene which is a bit longer than that originally. We shot a slightly longer scene that we later edited. Using what
would be the précis instead of verbatim. Just the way you'd read it in
the newspaper. We also wanted a trial scene in which they forgot the
trial and started to think about themselves, as people do, of course.
Eureka is a film in which everyone eventually thinks about
themselves.

*What other sources did you have in mind besides Marshall Houts's
book* King's X?

There are two or three books on Harry Oakes, one called *Who Killed Harry Oakes?* by James Leasor. *King's X* was a lawyer's account
of the trial, and it was from a legal perspective, none of which I used
at all.

Why was the Duke of Windsor part taken out?

I wrote it in an early draft, but the legal problems became too com-
plicated. It looked as if we weren't going to make the film before the
lawyers had sorted out the problems. Since it wasn't so important,
we took it out. The Duke of Windsor played an historically interesting role. He sided with the Germans during the war, and I
think Oakes might have as well.

Now you get on the topic that makes Eureka *very controversial: the
accusations of anti-Semitism.*

Why anti-Semitism?

*You are preoccupied with the gangster's Hebrew background, the
references to Kabbalah, the lit menorah that appears just before Mc-
Cann's murder, and the Wagnerian theme.*

The Jewish gangster is played by an Italian incidentally.

And the Italian is played by an Irishman.

Exactly. But the purpose of the menorah was to show the role of the
occult in various aspects of life. Now, for some reason, we are less
willing to admit that organized religion, whatever it is, has an occult
element to it. Of course it does! But because it is so traditional—praying to God, crossing yourself or putting on a silly
hat—we take it as natural. It isn't, of course. It's loony time. So, in

Eureka, we took God as if it were no different from devil worship or anything else. Mayakovsky relies on God to justify his evil ends. Everybody, you'll notice, has a kind of religious tone to them; except for Jack, and even he has a kind of vague Christian view when he says, "Do unto others as you would have them do unto you." We wanted to show that, underlying all behavior, is a religious attitude. We can't separate ourselves from it. And it is clear that many of the unpleasant things in life are done by people who have religious backgrounds.

You also set German romanticism against the Freudian view.

Yes. I personally was trying to go against Freudianism. I don't know if you ever can now. I wanted a sort of Balzacian view. Goethe's *Elective Affinities* is another influence. I wanted to convey the idea of people being attracted to and repelled by each other because of pure chemistry as opposed to psychology. But perhaps the film's more controversial side is the attitude towards gold, which is tied up with religion. There is a long-term relationship between gold and the occult. Whether you find the gold or sell it may be indicative of your religious persuasion. Gold is traditionally associated with Jews in terms of dealings, and so forth. I certainly wanted that aspect in it. It is not perhaps money that spawns this interest. Jews in South Africa were largely fascinated by gold, and these are perhaps not the best people on earth. After all, it's very hard to support that regime. And if we think about the connection between Jews and blacks in South Africa, we would have to come to some extremely unpleasant conclusions.

There are similar problems in America.

Yes, but South Africa is a very interesting case because the wealth in that country is to a very large extent Jewish, and the relationship between South Africa and Israel, for example, is a very interesting one when it comes to arms deals and other matters. However, I don't think anybody ever says that because it is something uncomfortable. But I like uncomfortable things. I would deny it as anti-Semitism, but I hold to the idea that, underneath all of these wheels and deals, there is a religious machinery. I don't think religion *did* it! I just feel it is interconnected in a way that cannot be unraveled. Also, I like religious images, that's taste. They are very powerful and interesting. I see no reason why one shouldn't use them, even summoning up forces, attitudes and feelings at the risk of not quite knowing where you are going.

McCann's wife reads the Tarot, which is derived from the Kabbalah.

And he comes from a place that is very superstitious.

Plus he is of Irish extraction; so we can assume he comes from a Roman Catholic background.

I did at one point have the Mayakovsky character actually want Hitler to win the war, which I am sure he did. Other Jews in the underworld felt the same, I'm sure, and still do. Look at what happened to Meyer Lansky. They wouldn't even let him into Israel. There has never before been a Jew refused entry into Israel.

Tell me a little about the other projects you and Roeg were supposed to tackle. I know about Miraclejack.

Miraclejack was a surreal psychodrama about a mystery man who leaps along skyscrapers and peers through windows. I wanted to involve a kind of audience participation in his voyeurism. The other was called *The Judge and His Hangman*, which was essentially a murder story. It was eventually filmed by Maximilian Schell and called *The End of the Game.* It had nothing to do with my script.

You also did a screenplay for J. G. Ballard's novel High Rise *That sounds like the ultimate Roeg-Mayersberg collaboration.*

I made it into a story about a man breaking into the building. He was a computer man. I placed it quite differently. In my version, the building existed in the middle of a desert in Arizona. It was like a totem. When he looked at it, he saw two buildings, but when he arrived there, he found only one. It was just a sight. People would come along, look at it, then go away again. Inside it there was just decay, and the man came in to try and find out what was going on. I delved into character vignettes, overlapping lives and relationships.

Like Chelsea Girls?

Something like that. It wasn't a project for Nic, though. Some producer came to me and asked me to write a script. He didn't like it. The rights reverted. Once again, it didn't fit the narrow genre

CONNUBIAL FOLLIES ON TUIN
AMANDA DONOHOE AND OLIVER REED FROM *CASTAWAY*

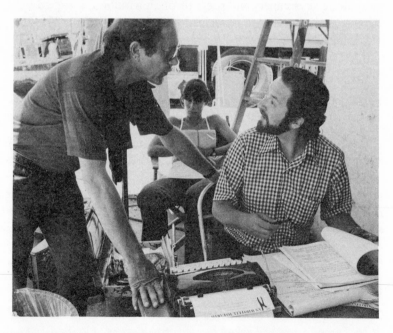

ROEG WITH SCREENWRITER PAUL MAYERSBERG ON THE SET OF
THE MAN WHO FELL TO EARTH

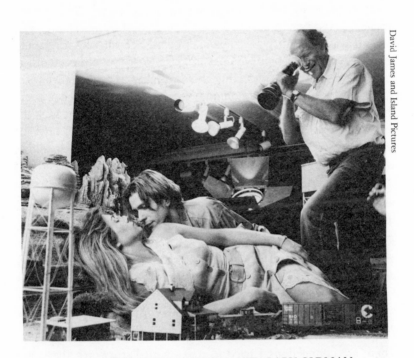

ROEG WITH THERESA RUSSELL AND GARY OLDMAN
ON THE SET OF *TRACK 29*

standards.

Your work touches on forbidden sexuality, with Merry Christmas, Mr. Lawrence *in particular.*

In *Mr. Lawrence*, I made a point of dealing with that, having a lot of remarks about it, which would have been uncharacteristic at the time. I don't think any English officer would have discussed homosexuality in 1943, and certainly no Japanese officer would discuss it even now. So, from a sociological point of view, it is totally false. It was more than just sexual. The story dealt with a relationship between two people who never spoke to or touched each other. It is a curious mixture of destiny and sensuality. It got bad reviews in America. People couldn't comprehend the relationships, nor could they understand why the Tom Conti character didn't fight back the way Rambo or Clint Eastwood would have. Instead, Conti says, ''I wish they'd stop hitting me.'' That is my favorite line. Such a thing is very puzzling to most Americans who think that they should just try to escape. But I suspect that few Korean or Vietnamese veterans have that view.

Then there is Farnsworth in The Man Who Fell To Earth. *Vito Russo, who wrote* The Celluloid Closet, *about gay images in movies, said that this is the only film he could think of which simply presented gay people without having to explain them. But I get a bad feeling at times, as if you are using Farnsworth as a metaphor for capitalism's sterility and that Peters, the black man, provides the miscegenation needed to revive it.*

There are connections I tried to make with Farnsworth that I am afraid to delve into now. He is very interesting. Nic and I wanted to have a man very much set in his ways but whose life would drastically change when Newton arrives. He couldn't be a family man because, after all, few patents lawyers are. He couldn't be with an old woman because that would have made him boring. If he were with a young woman then how could he be set in his ways? We tried to find a man whose life did not look as if it would change. He lived with this guy for a long time, and this was his life. Notice the way Farnsworth complains about his father while his lover Trevor embodies all of those fatherly characteristics.

You are fascinated by Japanese culture, which surfaces in some of your work.

Well, with *The Man Who Fell To Earth*, we put the Japanese elements in there because we thought they would attract someone who just arrived from another planet. Also, *"Don't Look Now"* never got shown in Japan, and Nic was very pissed off about that. We thought we'd get this film shown in Japan by cluttering it with Japanese motifs. The thing that Newton admires in the Japanese is the stillness and the symmetry. He loves the countryside and the stillness of natural things. But the thing that frightens him is the violence. The SONY television sets also drive him insane. So, there is another side of Japanese culture that destroys him. The Rip Torn character represents the darker, more aggressive side of sexuality. Notice when he goes to meet Newton, and the Japanese paper lantern starts to stir in the breeze. That's where the real psychodrama begins.

I like the fact that your films violate symmetry. You have a tendency to wedge in these peculiar subplots that throw people off. Do you think we'll be seeing more of that in movies?

Unfortunately no. I think it will remain a slightly outsiderish way. My feeling about audiences is that they are becoming more and more conventional in their demands. Meeting conventional demands is more important at the moment than meeting unconventional ones. People are not up for doubt now. We had some innovations in the past decade like Fassbinder, who is probably the only true original filmmaker in the seventies.

There are similarities between Fassbinder and Roeg. They both make their characters sensuous and cold at the same time.

I think it's the contradiction in character which makes them so interesting. When someone says a character is "cold," there is an aspect of the character revealed in the story that they didn't like. It is usually something in themselves which they recognize and despise. Somebody once asked me whom I identify with in *Hamlet*. There is a point in which it becomes one of those daft questions. Anyone who identifies with a character in *Hamlet* is in deep trouble.

As a screenwriter, how important a role do you feel dialogue plays? In all of Roeg's films, it seems very important.

When I use the word "image," I don't use it to denote just pictures. As far as I am concerned, the writing is the image too. Dialogue is the least of my worries. It is a process of constant refinement until you come down to just what you need. Mine is a very untheatrical style. Figures lurch from picture to picture, which is what I like, because it is very filmy.

For Eureka*'s murder scene, Roeg mentions that you simply wrote: "The Night of the Storm."*

I wrote a little more than that. But certainly the idea was to come up with a collection of images. Obviously, you cannot dictate certain areas of script until you're on location. You have to see whether the curtains will catch fire. When I'm working with Nic, I am able to leave certain areas sketchy. The blowtorch, the painting, the stairs will be in the script, but then he will create his own montage. That's not true with every scene but those scenes have to be done that way. I found that even for myself with writing and then directing *Captive* that I still left whole areas to be done.

In Captive, *you do something similar to* Eureka*'s trial scene by giving the camera a more self-effacing role.*

I've tried to make the scenes work in relation to one another as they pile up rather than intercut. There is an enormous number of mood switches to the point that it becomes kaleidoscopic. It is a montage of another kind. Going back to sexual ambiguity, I tend to use a lot of scenes where people dress and undress. I have an enormous number of masks and faces that are treated like masks. There are a lot of scenes in baths. You see people you wouldn't recognize in wet hair. There are only four characters, but they change all the time. It has to do with the fact that we don't recognize the patents of our behavior. We have one view of ourselves in the mirror and another view that other people have, and it is pathetic, the degree to which we persist in maintaining our own view of ourselves. In many respects, Oscar Wilde was right when he put so much importance on artifice. That's why I like art generally that is arty. I have no problem with artiness. There is a very thin line between pretension and subtlety. The use of art is precisely in its uselessness, not knowing what the fuck to make of it. I always believed in Jean Cocteau's dictum that if you have a work of art and know which way to hang it, it's not art.

"THE END . . .
AND THE BEGINNING . . . "

ROEG: I realize you're probably going to murder me by assembling my life and career into some kind of neat little order.

Maybe for the historians. You could be like a tragic hero who gets bumped off in the second act but really lives on.

That's what happens in *Eureka*. You think you've reached the peak, but there's left over life to kill. It brings us back to the illusions about time. How can you trace a person's life from one year to the next and be deluded into thinking you've mastered what they're about? I don't like to look back, as I've told you. I don't like to think about what I've done.

I hope I don't make you uncomfortable by asking you to recall anything embarrassing.

I've always tried to discourage chronology in my work.

But not entirely. There are still traces of it in all of your films. That's what makes them all the more puzzling.

You can never totally get away from it, I realize that. But when you're in the cutting room, you see how drastically you can change your perceptions and memories by rearranging the order of events. In *"Don't Look Now,"* you see an old lady, then you see a knife. But we can only infer that it's her knife that stabs the man. Whoever is in charge of editing a film really plays God. It's the juxtaposition of images that changes people's views. Pudovkin puts an empty plate in front of a fat man, and it means he's eaten; an empty plate in front of a thin man means he wishes he could have the food. Goebbels also realized this.

When you disrupt the chronology, you are accurately showing the human thought process.

That's especially true with *The Man Who Fell To Earth*. My whole film crew was so puzzled by what I was doing, and in a strange way, I think this helped the film. I wanted the story to be told through Newton's mind, how his thoughts could wander to the past, then the future, or even some point in time that never existed, until we're not sure where he is or where we are. Life isn't like *The Forsyte Saga* or a television mini-series where events tie neatly together with a little moral. Life is jagged, full of cross-references that aren't just coincidence. If you'll notice, the most interesting time reference in the film is the fact that Newton's camera innovation was only about five years ahead of our own technology. Today, self-developing film is nothing new. That's the ruse.

Do you believe in prophecy?

Yes. I think we get messages or warnings that we try to resist. Again, it has to do with our notions of time. I'd like to think there is a supernatural. I've never seen a UFO, but I must insist they exist. We are all haunted by our pasts. That's certainly true with most of my characters. You can't escape from the past, and you are always living out your future. But we usually don't know it. When you look into something like the Tarot, you can suddenly recognize the image of a dream when you're awake. There's no such thing as see-ing into the future because the future is already here. A premonition is just a way of confirming something you know. And I think film is the perfect medium to show this paradox. It's a time machine.

It's not as if our memories begin the moment we're born. They've existed beforehand, and that's sometimes a very difficult fact to cope with. It's like the broken glass in *"Don't Look Now"*:

so solid one moment, brittle the next. The important thing to remember about prophecy is that nothing ever stops. If you get an augury and it surfaces in real life years later, the two events are really one. The span between them means little.

You may have a semi-malevolent guardian angel.

I'm not sure. Usually, it works for me. When I'm in the middle of a project, and I want to get ideas together, I'm often able to stumble on a specific reference in a book by randomly opening to a passage. It's amazing how things can connect at an intense moment. It's magic, isn't it? While I planned *Castaway*, I came to a point when I got stuck. I wanted to add some new twist to the story, and I went through about three or four weeks of trying to figure it out. Then suddenly it came. I remembered Defoe and went back to *Robinson Crusoe*. It's funny how all of my films return to literature. I guess it's because all things are connected.

Our friend Charles Fort calls it "intermediatism."

Yes, I can see it now. If Fort were still alive, he would write: "In 1720, Defoe wrote *Crusoe*; in 1985, Roeg picked the book up. . . ."

* * *

ON THE SURFACE, CLIFF OWEN'S 1961 THRILLER *A PRIZE of Arms* looks like a precursor to TV's *Mission Impossible* or any Grade B potboiler with its detailed plot, clockwork pacing and obligatory suspense angles. As the film unfolds, three men attempt to rob a British Army payroll, experiencing one mishap after another as their calculated plans get slackened by army officials acting more out of bureaucratic pettiness than suspicion. However, about ten minutes into the movie, something odd happens . . .

As the men prepare to sneak into the army camp, their leader (Stanley Baker) steps towards the camera, his face in close-up, staring off into the foreground. One henchman, lurking behind, asks what is wrong. "I don't know," the leader replies. "There's something wrong somewhere. Something to do with rain." At this point, any viewers expecting a tightly packed action story are baffled but dubiously reassured when the leader (and the movie) regains consciousness and resumes the heist. Not until we get near the film's finale do we realize that the man's reverie lapse is actually a premonition of how the whole caper will fail. It is the previous night's rainfall that gives them away when the police find water-filled wheel marks and then deduce when and how the thieves had driven into the restricted area. The culprits do manage to steal the money, but their victory is short-lived when the leader finally establishes the connection that leaves the movie dangling.

Knowing that Roeg co-wrote this story, we are not surprised to find a seemingly linear yarn derailed by an ambiguous counterplot that raises out of place questions about psychic prophecy, not to mention grave doubts about the director's true motives. The fact that the thief is able to have a vision of rain hours before he understands what it means curbs the hair-trigger reflexes of audiences only prepared or willing to see a logical accumulation of causes and effects.

Now project yourself (in a manner similar to a Roeg flashforward) eight years later as *Performance*'s gangster Chas faces the thief's fatal dilemma. But, instead of failing to cover his tracks, he wanders into a pre-laid death trap after committing the murder that sends his own mob after him. Then we have John Baxter in *"Don't Look Now"* who refuses to heed the clairvoyant's warning as he walks along the labyrinthine canal where his killer waits. Or there is *Bad Timing*'s Alex Linden whose efforts to protect himself from complicity in his fiancée's drug overdose backfire when he is inconsistent about the exact number of hours elapsing between the time she swallows the pills and when he telephones for an ambulance. Similar fates vex many of Roeg's characters who think they are moving through linear time but, due to memory lapses and unconscious oversights, end up in vertigo.

Roeg's narrative mischief originates in these complex time games. Disjunct, uneven and frenetic, his stories flout continuity as events accelerate, slow down and intersect with little warning. Roeg provides us with a visual record of the human thought process as it fluctuates between mania and catatonia, full of paroxysmal images that sometimes multiply too fast for us to understand. Influenced by J. W. Dunne's forays into precognition, simultaneity and the maddening notion of ''infinite regress,'' Roeg conducts a jolting journey forward, backward and even sideways. Dunne's most notable books *An Experiment With Time* and *The Serial Universe* figure into much of Roeg's structure. With his inquiry into precognitive states, Dunne discovers an "associational network" between images in dreams with objects, people and events in waking life, finally concluding that, as experiences get displaced from their customary order, images of past and future blend, leaving even the most commonplace occurrences rife with paradox and deception. While Dunne's concepts are certainly not new in physics or fiction, Roeg is able to take them to the most outlandish extreme. He knocks his films out of shape, scrambling the order at the least expected or welcomed moments. When confronted by his spasmodic time machine, we can either stay frustrated and confused or, preferably, approach it with a demented circumspection.

> *We've gone too far . . . We haven't really gotten anywhere . . . We have to go much farther out . . . We have to go much further back, and faster . . .*
> —Turner and Pherber charting Chas's psychic excursion

Of all Roeg's oeuvre, *Performance* uses premonition and time-scrambling with the most racing and dizzying analogies. Its splintered montage forces us into our own time warp: the more rapid the juxtapositions, the more likely our minds lag behind as we try to establish a context.

Performance's lack of stylistic consistency is in keeping with the subject matter: the war between linear and tangential thinking. Chas begins by believing he is in full control of his destiny until he starts to see his time-line becoming frayed and jagged. We get a queasy sense of the forces manipulating him from the very first frames: aerial shots of the Rolls Royce carrying the lawyer out to indict Chas's mob crosscut with Chas roughing up a female sex partner prepare us for a later head-shaving ritual he performs on the lawyer's chauffeur, as well as the subsequent murder scenes when his taste for eroticized violence backfires.

The film's beginning sequences promise some kind of racy gangster tale as Chas fraternizes with his fellow hoods. But once he murders Joey Maddocks, Chas alters the story, entering Turner's human menagerie when the narrative takes its cataleptic stretch. Chas's world is asymmetrical. It is impossible to put him into a time-reversal and re-trace the steps to undo his mistake. This is because

Roeg and Cammell fill the story with auguries and images whose chronology is suspect. Even before Chas and Turner meet, Turner's image pops into the story to sabotage Chas's psyche, and we cannot delineate exactly when he takes control. Too many details overlap, many of which alternate between being actual events and hallucinations.

There are, however, parallels that hint of some consistency. Chas's fierce altercation in Harry Flowers's office, shortly before the Maddocks murder, resonates later when Turner, through a drug-induced dance ritual, forces Chas to see his past gangster antics as a sadomasochistic horror show. With a close-up of Turner applying red lipstick, we are reminded of the red dye Chas puts on his hair as part of his disguise, or the red ashtray Chas empties as his girlfriend dabs rouge on her cheek in the opening scene.

The story's complexity is congenial to Turner's universe which is much like those described in the Borges stories to which the film periodically refers as tales within a tale. *Tlön, Uqbar, Orbis Tertius* is the name given to a world with inverted natural laws, whose objects have no clear definition and whose nouns exist only as endless strings of adjectives. Preparing for his own imminent murder-suicide while Chas lurks in the basement like a waiting assassin, reads aloud from *The South*, which is about a convalescent who leaves his sanitorium for a train journey to an obscure province, engaging in a fatal knife fight pre-ordained the day he opens a volume of *The Thousand and One Nights*. But perhaps the most important story is *Death and the Compass*, which is never directly mentioned. Here, a police inspector tries to decipher an oracular series of homicides whose locations comprise a geometric puzzle, the final piece completed only when the inspector himself enters the murderer's carefully assembled lair. This is an understated allusion to *Performance*'s own geometric murder when Chas aims his gun precisely at the section of Turner's head that corresponds to the patch of hair Chas mysteriously leaves on the chauffeur's scalp. The connection becomes more obvious when Borges's photograph flashes in a shattered looking-glass as the camera takes us on a visceral tracking shot down Turner's punctured skull.

To understand how varied Roeg's treatment of time can be, we have only to compare *Performance* to *Walkabout*, which is less frantic but just as ellipitical. *Walkabout* reduces the conflict between linear and psychic time to what seems to be a remake of the Genesis tale. The aborigine goes on his "walkabout" to obtain some continuity with his environment, but, after meeting up with the lost children, loses his innocence and will to survive.

Walkabout reinforces its circular theme by framing the story with cross-references between past and future. The insurmountable wall at the beginning and end could be circumscribing either the wilderness or the city; and by the end of the film, we realize both places are a prison. Opening shots of soldiers marching through Sydney prepare us for a later close-up of the young girl stomping on the concrete when she and her brother leave the aborigine for the road back to their civilization. There is also the eerie music that accompanies the initial city scenes and recurs with the aborigine's death dance. Time spans also merge when the father's suicide (ultimately linked to the aborigine's death) liberates a chain of ominous portents: the ants grazing the food left over from the children's aborted picnic reappear on the aborigine's corpse; the numerous maggot-ridden carcasses left in the sand are a sardonic reminder of an earlier scene when the children's mother prepares a roast; jump-cuts between the aborigine killing game and a butcher chopping meat foreshadow the climactic animal slaughter, the sight of which propels the aborigine into his funereal rite.

Roeg repeatedly breaks story continuity with abrupt zooms and other camera pyrotechnics which may seem apropos to the isolated objects, faces and body parts along the city streets, but are more disconcerting and incongruous in the nature setting. Once they are in the outback, the children experience what Chas must feel when delivered into Turner's clutches. Time distends. The children are guided only by their transistor radio whose battery life is guaranteed for 400 hours. But the longer the children remain stranded, the more each sunrise looks like the next and the more it appears to us that the father's suicide and the aborigine's later death are essentially the same event converging.

They all want a lot of mumbo jumbo about ectoplasm and holding hands. Second sight is a gift from the good Lord, who sees all things; and I consider it an impertinence to call his creatures from rest for our entertainment.

—The psychic makes her pitch
to contact the Baxters' dead child

While *Walkabout* relates a somber, humanistic story, *"Don't Look Now"* snares us into a metaphysical web. On the one hand, the film is much in keeping with a recognizable thriller, with shades of Poe, Conan-Doyle and an even more decadent Hitchcock. But we are never certain if the prophecies and time traps have occult or causal explanations.

"Don't Look Now" begins with the Baxters at home in England. The children play by the backyard pond while John and Laura are inside, oblivious to any approaching danger. While studying slides of the Venice cathedral he is hired to restore, John is preoccupied with one of a red-hooded figure kneeling in a pew with its back toward the camera. As the image flashes, Laura looks up from a book and asks: "If the world is round, why is a frozen pond flat?" When John is unable to answer, Laura finds in her encyclopedia that flatness is just an illusion and that lakes actually curve. John, in turn, replies: "Nothing is what it seems"—a limp response considering that the book prompting Laura's question is one he had written entitled *Beyond the Fragile Geometry of Space*. From that moment on, the story's death auguries start multiplying just when John accidentally spills water on the slide. Upon seeing the slide's hooded figure blister and assume an odd shape, he is impelled to check on the children just as Roeg cuts to a shot of Christine drowning in the pond.

Like *Performance*, *"Don't Look Now"* comprises a mystifying visual pattern with numerous red images: the daughter's raincoat; the person in the slide; the robe worn by a hotel tenant who discovers John lurking; a handkerchief the psychic fondles; and even the tinted base of the glass John drinks from while hearing news of his son's injury.

To engage us further, Roeg assembles contours that have vague similarities: the blistering slide (seen during the drowning and after John's murder) resembles the position of Christine's body when

John lifts her out of the water, which, in turn, looks something like the brooch one of the sisters keeps pinned to her blouse. These resemble the shape of the mosaic for which John almost dies trying to restore, or the map appearing in the background as the police chief listens to John's missing persons report. Each object finally approximates the shape of a fetus which, as the film implies, may replace Christine or another child that the sisters claim to have also lost. Roeg uses this pregnancy theme as another time teaser, suggesting a gestation process whose span is not clear. When was the conception? Which child is it? Why do we overhear a crying baby during the seance while the psychic feigns labor pains? Roeg himself hints that this *Rosemary's Baby* entity may be conceived when the Baxters enact a simultaneous love and death ritual at their hotel shortly before their initial encounter with the hooded killer. This moment of intimacy and impending doom is made even more tenuous by Roeg's crosscutting between the lovemaking and shots of the Baxters, in separate rooms, dressing for dinner: John looks apprehensive while Laura, for the first time, seems serene as she strokes her womb area. We can also trace this idea back to the film's credits which furnish a background dissolving from the pond where Christine drowns to the bathroom window of the Venice hotel which appears just before the Baxters make love.

Roeg incorporates time ambivalence into minute scenic details to give us the sense of an older world waiting to vindicate itself against new invaders. The Baxters' house is an awkward combination of modern and Tudor style. In one instance, we cut from an ancient wall, which John attempts to repair, to Laura writing a letter with a Rapidograph pen. When the Baxters visit a Gothic cathedral, John nervously fiddles with an out-of-place electric light switch.

An even more bizarre time trick occurs after Laura leaves Venice to attend to the injured son. Preparing to join her, John discovers Laura, the son and the two sisters floating past him on a vaporetto which, by the film's conclusion, we find is actually his own funeral cortège. John's temporal loop leads him to a displaced encounter with his future self. Searching the city for the women, he comes across a stray glove (identical to the pair he is wearing) by the canal where he will die. After tracing his steps back to the sisters' hotel, he finds only a painting they had left behind of three women and a child—another reference to the funeral boat.

Only during the final seconds before the dwarf bludgeons him
does John finally connect the image on the slide with that of his
killer. Even with these last frantic moments of revelation, seen
through a montage of flashbacks, the story's mosaic, like the one in
the church, resists completion.

> *The strange thing about television is that it doesn't tell you*
> *everything. It shows you everything there is to know about*
> *life on earth. Yet the mysteries remain.*
> —Newton realizing that his prime
> information source is flawed.

Newton's description of television is also apt for *The Man Who
Fell To Earth*'s style as it bombards us with layers of images and
allusions designed to go nowhere. This film brings Roeg's time
obsession to new complexities and absurdities. Like the Walter Tevis
novel, the film portrays an alien caught in an earthbound existence.
The Man Who Fell To Earth is essentially constructed from the
viewpoint of extraterrestrial abductees who report vast chunks of
time missing from their memories after being captured. Only now,
we are the ones abducting the alien. Like the hapless figure in Edwin
Abbott's classic novel *Flatland*, who vainly tries to explain his two-
dimensional existence to one-dimensional beings, Newton's percep-
tual conflicts arise when he mentally traverses through four dimensions but remains physically confined to three.

Entering Newton's mind, we are forced to come to terms with a
world that seems familiar on the surface, but whose context is absent. To convey this confusion, Roeg purposely fashions an abstruse
story structure that makes enormous time leaps. Days, years, even
decades elapse sporadically and inconsistently. We are uncertain as
to how long it takes Newton, from the moment he lands, to amass
his fortune, patent his product, build his corporation, get sabotaged
and finally escape from his captors.

For Newton, past, present and future are interchangeable, but not
necessarily reversible, as we later learn when he fails to return to his
origins. Visions of his space family seem as illusory as the television
commercial he makes in an attempt to re-visit his past identity. To
complicate matters, Roeg makes time conflict even among the
humans who grow old at different rates while Newton remains

ageless, obviously cut off from the rhythm of his surroundings.

The Man Who Fell To Earth is also imbued with an eerie anthropology: part nostalgia and part amnesia. Here, we get a taxidermic history of media images and kitsch. Whenever any of the characters seem ready to break out into the present, Roeg conjures a pastiche of movie references, old pop songs and maudlin soundtracks to destroy any potential realism. Relics and artifacts creep into the landscape as reminders of eras that have come and gone before us or of a past which may never have happened. Newton lands in a barren town full of dilapidated buildings, junk railways and abandoned amusement rides. Among his first human encounters is an elderly curio dealer whose excessive wrinkles are as much an emblem of time's passage as the Louis Armstrong rendition of "Blueberry Hill" that plays in the background. Oliver Farnsworth, Newton's first companion and business partner, lives in an apartment decorated in a haphazard combination of Victorian, Art Deco and ultra-modern motifs. The house Newton later builds for himself —mixing ancient Japanese with high-tech—is equally devoid of a stable time period, much like the portable mud-hut that is supposed to be the futuristic train on his home planet.

Without a navigable course, *The Man Who Fell To Earth* takes us on a trip that amalgamates different periods and places. While at a restaurant, Newton is appalled by the violence of a Kabuki ritual as well as by one of Bryce's sexual exploits occurring far away, the cacophony of both events merging into a single noise. In the first of many flashbacks to his planet (which may also be a post-holocaust earth), Newton envisions his family running through a grassy field, which then turns into an Impressionistic landscape and finally a barren desert. Newton later teleports himself before a pioneer family that looks back at him as his limousine rides along a highway. Once he is incarcerated, we are led to him through a tracking shot inside several rooms, each depicting the styles of cultures at their apogee, finally leading to the cold boredom of pop art and a *trompe l'oeil* nature setting grafted onto wallpaper.

More so than any other Roeg film, *The Man Who Fell To Earth* has portents that seem deliberately vague and fanciful. The most subtle example is a glare of refracted sunlight linking events leading to Newton's downfall: 1) just as Newton takes his first drink of earth water; 2) in a photograph in Farnsworth's office when Bryce formally introduces himself to Newton's corporation and which later appears outside of Newton's desert hideaway when Bryce arrives to uncover the true alien identity; and 3) grazing across the black government agent's naked buttocks as he dives triumphantly into his pool after seizing Newton's power.

During his visit, Newton becomes fixated on trains and television—two symbols of our planet's space and time myopia. Unlike the train on Newton's planet which seems to ride on an eternal loop, our railways span immense areas but never connect in infinity. The train motif recurs throughout with locomotive sounds carefully embedded in the soundtrack. We hear a steam engine and see its decrepit ghost in the background as Newton makes his messianic descent in the beginning; again, when Mary-Lou carries him (in Pietà fashion) into his hotel room after he faints. The image haunts Newton till the very end when, in a desperate attempt to contact his dead wife, he records an album with a jacket sleeve depicting a speeding train frozen in time.

A slight hint of order emerges when Newton escapes from prison. We hear a din of ticking clocks and ringing bells, but their noise suddenly conforms to a sing-songy pattern as he descends in the elevator to his dubious freedom. Once Newton is used up and abandoned, the mystery is not solved, but is at least contained by those in charge. Also, Newton's travels from New York and Chicago to the Southwest suggest a geomantic triangle inside of which Newton's fate is already sealed.

The fact that Newton gets most of his knowledge from television also accounts for the film's open-ended style. Roeg makes every attempt to portray his protagonist as video culture's supreme whipping boy, even to the extent of tinting Newton's hair a near fluorescent red, in the very first scene, to imply that, besides getting inconclusive information, he may have all along been watching earth through distorted color reception.

> *How we come into this world and how we go out is different
> for every one of us. We are constantly in isolation:
> watching, spying on everyone and everything around us. In
> birth, chance seems to be merely the visible part of an as yet
> unknown and uncomprehended natural law . . .*
>   —Alex Linden addressing his students

With *Bad Timing*, the words ''flashback'' and ''flashforward''
are misnomers. All time exists in a vacuum, no matter how linear or
realistic the story may seem. Here, Roeg fuses two narratives: one
taking place over the span of five months as Alex and Milena's affair
evolves from idle interest to obsession; the other occurs over five
hours when Milena swallows the pills and Alex must grapple with
the detective Frederich Netusil's suspicions of foul play. But the
story is less concerned with supposed ''actual'' doings and more involved with Alex and Frederich as they try to interpret events with
their paranoid logic, making us unsure which viewpoint is which.

Performance distorts its time frame by digressing from Chas's
diurnal gangster life to Turner's dream world; *The Man Who Fell
To Earth* ruptures its chronology in order to justify its fantastic plot;
but *Bad Timing* is much more devious by hoodwinking us with a
relentlessly realistic veneer. There are no direct supernatural
references, yet the story crosses that flimsy boundary between social
science and occultism. Like Freud and Rank, who enumerate their
own subjective phobias under the guise of science, Alex and
Frederich's belief systems grow more fantastic and unreliable as the
episodes surrounding Milena's overdose get more inexact. The further they investigate, the more impalpable the pattern. Even when
Frederich tries to make Alex re-live the order of events, not a shred
of the testimony is conclusive. We never know whether Alex is attempting to tell the truth or Frederich is superimposing his own version of the story. The most the two men can do is quibble over exact
points on the clock's minute hand: what time Alex receives
Milena's call; when he leaves for her apartment; the length of
Milena's toxic process; and the hour Alex finally phones for an ambulance.

When Alex is interrogated, the film switches to the supposedly actual circumstances which often contradict his words. For example,
he contends that he does not remember the precise time of Milena's

suicide call, yet a following scene has him looking at his watch after hanging up the receiver.

Bad Timing is a race that we enter at both the start and the finish. It opens with Alex and Milena sauntering through an Austrian gallery, each in their separate worlds as the distorted subjects in the paintings stare back at them as taunting harbingers of their romance. Suddenly, we switch to a speeding ambulance with Alex inside, huddled over Milena's unconscious body. As Milena's faint voice-over intones, "Stefan, I'm sorry. . . ," Roeg cuts to Stefan, Milena's Czech husband, bidding her a laconic and painful farewell at the Bratislava Bridge as she goes to live in Vienna. This somber and expanded interlude, besides being a radical departure from the film's predominantly hectic pace, triumphs paradoxically because it adds too much detail too soon. Then, instead of leveling off to help us digest the contrasting scenes, the film continues to bombard us with unfinished business.

While avoiding outright prophecies, Roeg still includes a foreshadowing of the lovers' schism. During their first argument, Milena holds Paul Bowles's *The Sheltering Sky*, a story about a doomed love that takes place in Morocco, which prepares us for the moment in Marrakesh when Milena spurns Alex's marriage proposal. In another instance, when Milena visits Alex at the Freud Institute where he teaches, she pulls Alex onto a replica of Dr. Freud's couch and asks, "Is there hope for us, doctor?" Alex replies "No," but in a subsequent scene, while waiting to hear whether Milena survives, he reconstructs the encounter in his mind, changing his answer to "Yes" in an attempt to exonerate himself.

Roeg constantly reminds us that Alex's erotic overtures are really repressed aggressions when he intercuts their lovemaking with shots of Milena's tracheotomy. The same clocks we hear in *The Man Who Fell To Earth*, when Newton is rendered useless, return as Alex hovers over Milena's near-corpse after he extracts all that he wants out of her.

The one thread in the film which threatens to tie the loose ends is Alex and Milena's taped telephone conversation made the night of the suicide. The dialogue sounds different each time, alternating from a seemingly real to a pretend suicide threat. Like the Bratislava Bridge scene whose actual chronological place is indeterminate, these taped voices have no exact origin, but could be snippets of other conversations, or even other suicide threats which turn this latest trauma from a climax to a tautology. We may feel impelled to keep mental notes of the various clocks that flash throughout the film, but the proper time really does not matter. The characters' interpretations, as well as our own, are the final reality.

> *Do you know what eternity looks like? It's white, and yet very dark, like a desert of snow in the night. Now I've reached the edge of eternity, the abyss, nothing . . . Once I had it all; now I just have everything . . .*
> —Jack McCann reciting his eulogy

After abandoning his partners to strike gold on his own, Jack McCann arrives at a claims office where another dazed prospector, barefoot and frostbitten, warns "It's the end," before firing a pistol into his mouth. Jack, half mad with his quest, can only watch the suicide impassively, replying, "It's not over until it's over"—a tautology that is the key to *Eureka*'s circular reasoning. Within the first half hour or so, the film ends and begins again, just as in *Bad Timing*, only with allegorical overtones.

It is an alchemist's scenario: Jack acquires a magic stone which guides him to what he thinks is the real discovery, but as his former lover Frieda, a clairvoyant gypsy, looks into her crystal ball, we see the fire leading to the treasure and ultimately to his grisly immolation two decades later. Jack's real gold is not the alloy but the self-awareness that comes with dying.

Despite its asymmetry, *Eureka* is fraught with structural consistencies, images that mirror each other as we follow Jack through his ecstasy and demise. The suicidal prospector's shattered head dissolves into fireworks that reappear after Jack's decapitation; a golden chain Jack uses as a symbolic link to his daughter Tracy ends up in the hands of his hated son-in-law Claude, only to fall into Jack's hands again on the night of his murder, which Claude foresees during a voodoo ceremony. Roeg makes his different characters mouth similar lines and assume similar positions to induce déjà vu. Even Jack's moment of triumph anticipates his violent death as the gold fluid spits him in a cosmic rejection from the earth's bowels.

Structurally, *Eureka* recalls *Performance*, with its semblance of an adventure succeeded by tortuous and morbid contemplation. When he returns to celebrate his victory, Jack finds Frieda nearing death, struggling to give him her final prophecy which summarizes his life as "the end . . . and the beginning . . ." Suddenly, Frieda's fireplace emits a spark which jumps into the future onto Jack's lap when he is back in the Yukon twenty years later, reminiscing to Tracy about his exploits. From here on, the story is purposely designed as an ongoing anticlimax. In Frieda's words, Jack has "plenty of left over life to kill," devoid of a purpose and prey to a horde of acquisitive associates waiting to appropriate all he wins. He may dig up his treasure in the snow, but chooses to live out his last days in the Caribbean, as if inadvertently seeking to recapture an elemental balance capsized by his Yukon venture.

Jack parallels *"Don't Look Now"*'s Baxter, an agnostic who fails to heed his death omens while surrounded by a cabal of believers. Jack's wife Helen ponders over her Tarot deck (obsessed by the Hanged Man card); his son-in-law Claude shares with the gangster Mayakovsky and the shady lawyer DiMatto an interest in the Kabbalah. Jack also lives in a country whose inhabitants are steeped in voodoo rituals that may also play a role in his destruction. *Eureka* also uses *"Don't Look Now"*'s gestation theme with Jack's alchemical stone harboring a fetus, similar to the one in John Baxter's slide, whose light dies out on the night of the murder. *Eureka*'s whole story becomes a metaphorical abortion once Jack exits and Tracy takes his place. From then on, the film's rhythm is traumatized by a long and grueling courtroom scene in which *Eureka*'s adventure crystallizes into a purely philosophical debate, a juncture preparing us for the more stagnant idea exchange that occurs in *Insignificance* as time stops and contemplation begins.

> *Did you know that according to the Law of Probability, you drink a glass of water and you drink a piece of Napoleon's crap? Perhaps Mussolini's, but more likely Napoleon's on account of he's been dead longer.*
> —The Senator's rendition of Einstein's law

After so many harrowing forays on and through the clock, Roeg perhaps sees himself as Jack McCann, looking for some respite after trembling so long over the precipice. *Insignificance* may seem less abstruse because of Roeg's fealty to the film's main star, The Professor (or Albert Einstein), who prefers safer predictions over the more inscrutable and random world of quantum physics.

In *Insignificance*, Roeg leaps back and forth between past, present and possibly future, without really disorienting anyone. This is partly because the film sets itself up with the subject of space-time as its central discourse, leaving no surprises. There is Roeg's familiar use of recurrent images: a gliding wristwatch warning and reminding us of the fatal nuclear hour; flowing curtains and bedsheets contrasted with a cerement covering bomb victims; split-second scenes of the Hiroshima aftermath preparing us for the final holocaust sequence—all neatly adding up to a predictable finale. The Actress may be able to foresee another miscarriage, or The Professor may imagine a world-wide nuclear hecatomb, but these are variations on events that will already happen. Even the film's uncanny premise, of being able to unite four of America's legends under one roof, is also from the vantage point of us spectators safely looking back some thirty years after the fact.

However, Roeg realizes this limitation and solves the problem by compounding it. If we are doomed to look at events through the rosy perspective of *Life* magazine, then the film should likewise reduce the era and the people to two-dimensional images. Just as in *The Man Who Fell To Earth*, when we could only see American culture through media fabrication, *Insignificance* presents the paragons of beauty, brains, power and fame just as they are registered by our television-weaned synapses. Roeg even uses the washed-out, artificial colors found in fifties picture postcards to imply how much our vision is commodity house-trained.

Unlike Baxter, Newton, McCann and other characters preceding him, The Professor is haunted by a doomsday for which he is consciously prepared. *Insignificance*'s horror is inevitable and documented. Thus, the film's core message—our inability to stop time and repair past mistakes—is mired more in calculation than prophecy.

While *Insignificance* converts the subject of time into a parlor chat between "knowing" parties, *Castaway* reduces it further to an ongoing marital squabble. Gerald and Lucy arrive on the Isle of Tuin and immediately retreat into separate mental worlds. Gerald, dejected and sexually famished, constantly refers to clocks and moon

variations to keep track of the passing days; while Lucy, enamored
with her tropical surroundings, loses all awareness of time and has to
be informed when their one-year experiment finally terminates. The
time conflict in *Walkabout* is absent here because Lucy has no desire
to return to the old life. Even Gerald's preoccupation with clocks is
more out of boredom than concern. If anything, time is just a
taunting reminder of a mating cycle long overdue. In one scene,
Gerald stumbles upon a pair of Lucy's panties left hanging from a
tree. His first randy reaction is: "It's been that long?" Lucy also
notices that her periods stop, due to malnutrition, as she fumbles
with an ashy stone that looks like a dead fetus.

Roeg's repeated references to desiccated embryos, stillbirths,
miscarriages and infertility reveal another time thread which, in
some ways, may be his most salient. The cycles of regeneration are
nature's most inescapable prison. So, we are not surprised to find
Roeg's work betraying constant misgivings about insemination and
pregnancy. The relief that Pherber and Lucy feel in *Performance*
when they both learn that Chas did not "screw" either of them is
tantamount to the revulsion Mary-Lou exhibits in *The Man Who
Fell To Earth* as Newton's semen ejaculates from his pectorals like
some lethal virus. *Walkabout*'s equation of female pudenda with a
barren tree echoes in *Eureka* with the suggestion that Tracy is
unable to have a child and, of course, in *Insignificance* with The Actress whose battered womb cannot hold a baby. The fetus in *"Don't
Look Now"* survives only once the father is neutralized; just as
Jack's embryonic stone in *Eureka* assumes an even stronger supernatural presence when it sets on his mantelpiece like a lacquered
abortion.

Often, Roeg supplies sinister sexual metaphors, providing a visual
counterpart to Andrea Dworkin's nightmare visions of procreative
coupling. The malevolent wind-machine aiming at The Actress'
derrière, the speculum invading Milena on the operating table, the
juxtaposed scenes of the girl swimming naked with the aborigine
spearing fish—all indicate that sexual conquest leads to another ir-
reversible time trap.

We may be able to gauge this touch-and-cringe attitude toward
sex by watching the figurative rape transpire through Newton's
television sets in *The Man Who Fell To Earth* after he and Mary-
Lou have their first domestic brawl. As Mary-Lou stands in front of

the army of screens in a futile attempt to compete with them for her lover's attention, Newton sits at the video control panel (which looks like a dentist's chair) playing the role of a lecher about to give and receive sweet pain. The images catching his eye begin with such pre-coital niceties as a woman dutifully kneeling in front of her man; a prostrate lioness waiting to be mounted; a camera roving along a row of crossed female legs in a classroom while, on another screen, Elvis Presley serenades a phalanx of female admirers. Then, as the lions start fucking, Elvis's entourage starts swooning, and a clip from the film *Billy Budd* appears with a ship's crew preparing to execute its innocent sailor, Newton spurns the images, crying out "Leave my mind alone." Soon, coitus becomes carnage as the top lion climaxes; Stacy Keach brutalizes a karate opponent from the film *End of the Road*; Elvis wrests his phallic microphone back from his wenches; a deer is devoured; Billy Budd hangs; and a sadistic pilot "pulls the stick" to unleash a stream of bombs from his fighter plane.

The visual cacophony is a time-traveler's survey of the American lust for power that thrives on symbols of feminine submission. Newton, in turn, is another of the sacrificial lambs, and the images he tries to get out of his mind are actually omens of another kind of rape awaiting *him*.

Perhaps Roeg's precious tendency to obscure time and make his storylines crumble just when we expect them to tie together is a symbolic snub at the mechanics of fucking, from which our climax-directed narrative traditions probably originate.

Roeg's most optimistic moments occur when his characters avoid the mating rut altogether and escape into a narcissistic universe that is timeless and static. Lucy, in *Castaway*, is happiest when left to herself on the island just as the alien Newton envisions a love act which lets him wallow in his own semen without having to resort to penetration. It also seems that, as Roeg advances, his experiments with time get more outwardly sexual until, with *Track 29*, they become localized in his testicles through his main character Martin, and, more importantly, in his uterus through Linda.

*We were very close, very close once upon a time. As close as
close can be. Do you not remember the tug of my lips on
your tender young breast?*

—Martin courting ''Mummy''

As *Track 29* unfolds, Martin's metamorphosis from a child into
an adult, and vice versa, occurs more through behavioral than
physical changes. The narrative has similar tricks as those employed
in *The Man Who Fell To Earth* with people's indeterminate ages
and the symbol of passing trains to signify unaccountable time
lapses. When Martin arrives in Wilmington, he is in essence a per-
mutation of Newton. But *Track 29*'s time discourse is more biology
than philosophy, with a narrative resembling the growth stages of a
quirky boy. Linda, whom Martin accuses of being his mother, looks
his exact age, and their supposed familial relationship looks more
dubious as they become more sexually immersed.

Roeg further obscures the story's time period by having sixties
cartoon images like Tennessee Tuxedo, King Leonardo and
Bullwinkle appear on Linda's TV screens, even though we are supposed to be in the eighties. In one instance, Martin meets up with a
truck driver who appears to be an older version of himself, sporting
the same duck-tail haircut that Martin's supposed father wears when
we flash back to Linda's rape.

Linda's personality also changes drastically from that of a neurotic
housewife to a giddy adolescent with a school crush. While the film
seems to tailor itself according to Martin's hormonal alterations,
Linda's viewpoint assumes more importance in the same manner
that Milena's enigmatic perspective in *Bad Timing* forces us to
question the men who try to dominate the narrative with their own
time-schemes. But now, the female protagonist, instead of being
sterile, is vexed by her fertility. Martin returns with memories of a
conception that should or may never have happened. It is as if Linda
is an incarnation of *''Don't Look Now'''*s Laura who comes face to
face with her demon child.

Linda's husband Henry, in turn, uses his obsession for toy trains
as an excuse to alienate Linda and to revert to some infantile stage of
his own. The diorama he constructs around his train set is, in fact, a
replica of the abandoned Haneyville station that Newton enters
when *The Man Who Fell To Earth* begins. Only now, it is fully

restored as part of Henry's "picture of long ago when we knew who we were." Throughout the film, Henry envisions trains running straight ahead, crosswise, backwards and in circles, but all the while, he expects Linda to be the symbolic tunnel through which the tracks plunge. Finally, when Henry declares that "women and trains don't mix," he betrays a father-son complicity nurtured by a shared disdain for the family "whore." But Martin, the vengeful imp, also longs to destroy the train set (and its embodiment of Henry's demented dream) in the same manner he seeks to pummel and gnaw at his mother.

Screenwriter Dennis Potter creates Linda maybe to atone for the excessive misogyny of his character Philip Marlow in *The Singing Detective*. Marlow, immobilized in a hospital bed, is beleaguered by past demons (most of them female) responsible for his anger and guilt. As his story continues, we start to suspect that some of the events spill over from the ongoing murder mystery he composes in his head. Linda, likewise, exists between fiction and non-fiction as she descends into a similar purgatory of flashbacks leading to a murder which, like a Rorschach blot, is as real as you choose to make it.

When finally confronted with unavoidable battles of conscience, survival and lust, *Track 29*'s Linda must take control of the narrative and actually *use* Martin as a key to re-set the clock. She mates with her progeny and regresses to the monster's gestation—a journey which brings Roeg's cause-and-effect puzzle full circle. To outdo the thief in *A Prize of Arms* (who cannot go back to undo his deadly error), Linda must re-trace her steps, via the fallopian tube, to the moment of her total submission—back to the beginning, only to wind up at the end and into a limbo that confirms Borges's parable about life inside a vast, circular library *"whose exact center is any one of its hexagons and whose circumference is inaccessible."*

DOPPELGÄNGERS: DAVID BOWIE AND RIP TORN

DOPPELGÄNGER CAMP: ROEG WITH CRITIC JOHN SIMON

THE FUGITIVE VIEWPOINT

When someone asked you why you put the mysterious onlooker in The Man Who Fell To Earth, *you repled that "We are all being watched."*

ROEG: Yes, I think that's an important idea. We *are* being watched, if not by other people, then by ourselves, which can be even worse.

What about the Third Man *theme in both* The Man Who Fell To Earth *and* Bad Timing?

No matter what you do, you are always accountable to another person. Someone is formulating your life from an angle you may know little about.

I'm thinking of the scene in Bad Timing *when Alex questions that mysterious man in the café . . .*

He was played by Daniel Massey, Raymond Massey's son.

He says: "What I say has to be taken in the context of who I am."

Exactly. He was talking about Stefan, Milena's husband. If you ask someone a question about someone else, what happens is you usually adjust the opinion to suit *your* opinion. You eliminate the middle man who is the very person you're interviewing. If you ask a liar about someone, "Do you think he'll shit on me?" and the liar says, "No," you say, "Good." But then the man might say, "But do you know who *I* am?" And I made a point of having the man sexually ambivalent, so that you can't tell whether he is fancying Alex. Yes, the *Third Man* idea was deliberate.

That may explain why you film characters from behind. You especially like to photograph the backs of their heads.

It's a cruel vantage point, isn't it? You always know there has to be someone behind watching the person you cannot see. People are often most interesting at their most vulnerable.

There are also people lurking in the shadows, like the black men in Performance.

Yes. In the sixties, that's how white people saw them. They were there, but like shadows. Why make a point of it when they weren't a point? They were shadows; so that's how I depicted them. But no matter where you go, there are always people lurking about . . .

* * *

Who is the third who walks always behind you?
When I count, there are only you and I together
But when I look ahead up the white road
There is always another walking beside you
Gliding wrapt in a brown mantle, hooded
I do not know whether a man or woman
—But who is that on the other side of you?

THIS PASSAGE FROM T. S. ELIOT'S "THE WASTE LAND" gives an almost faithful description of the alien's descent in the beginning of *The Man Who Fell To Earth*. It also suggests the fugitive, inscrutable third eye that creeps into every Roeg story. Like the Eliot poem, *The Man Who Fell To Earth* is about a world barren and anesthetized by its self-consciousness and impotence. This solitude blossoms into paranoia when the loner, far from being the center of the universe, is more than ever vulnerable to outside intrusion. As our solitude increases, the alien outside of us grows larger.

When Newton descends the hill, the mysterious man who watches him from behind disappears, only to resurface at Newton's bedside years later. We are never given any further elucidation about his identity or the part he plays in the conspiracy. Nor can we track down the sinister truck driver who follows Newton each time he goes to Haneyville and later reappears in *Track 29* to pursue Martin in North Carolina. A similar mystery occurs in *Performance* when the only other person witnessing Chas and Turner's psychic melding (during the Maddocks murder) is a marginal character who leaves the scene of the crime and is never heard from again. What should we make of the brooding Italian woman in *"Don't Look Now"* who loiters in the lavatory as the psychic makes her initial contact with Laura's dead daughter? Or even the seemingly insignificant frump in *Castaway* creeping in the background of the hotel lobby when Gerald and Lucy meet on their "ultimate blind date"?

Roeg habitually places some of the story's most valuable information and most tender moments in view of a fleeting figure who runs away with the goods. We, in turn, discover ourselves trying to analyze and extrapolate on a world we cannot fully perceive because it is anterior to the film's frame.

Roeg's fugitive viewpoint reverts again to J. W. Dunne, who points out the dangers resulting when time eludes our conscious control, and we must imagine ourselves at the whim of temporal laws more complete than our own. Dunne envisions an "infinite regress" that occurs when our perceived time is monitored by a more complex system which, in turn, is monitored by another, ad infinitum. Roeg's narratives, likewise, are much like Dunne's parable of the mad artist who attempts to paint a picture of the universe but must always step back to include himself painting the picture, then step back again, and again.

Rather than strive for a unifying vision in the face of these countless obstacles, Roeg prefers to obscure the references even more. He sandwiches a multitude of viewpoints inside of a larger context so vast that it is even out of *his* control. Indeed, he is not at all skittish about wedging himself into the many layers which can be likened to a Chinese box tipped on its axis, its serial order no longer recognizable. Perhaps this is the message in *Performance* when Chas, after chatting on the telephone with his friend Tony about the

need for a ''new image,'' opens Turner's closet to a collection of
empty picture frames piled on top of each other. Or in *Walkabout*
when the little boy tells the aborigine a story while book pages turn
in the foreground, a reminder that we are seeing not only a story
within a story, but all of reality reconstituted through an alien
medium that denies us direct access.

Sleight of hand editing also abounds. In *''Don't Look Now''*,
when Laura tries to explain to John why the psychic is genuine,
Roeg cuts to a shot of the sisters laughing hysterically, making us
wonder if the Baxters are being defrauded after all. Also, in the
seance scene, Roeg calls attention to the women rearranging their
legs under a table, yet does not explain what the gesture means. The
doctors in *The Man Who Fell To Earth* examine Newton on an
operating table, but the camera is careful not to show exactly what
they are looking for or may have found. Do they discover alien
signs? Or are they maybe grafting another disguise onto his body?
Such scenes beg other questions: Why does Newton's spacecraft
land in a lake while Newton emerges from a hilltop far away from
the landing site? What can we glean from the constant construction
occurring outside of Newton's prison? Why does Newton escape
from his confinement, descend in a long elevator ride, walk out into
a hotel lobby, then exit from a building that appears little more than
two stories high?

Bad Timing and *Eureka* provide further discontinuities. *Bad
Timing* never really tells us whether Alex rapes Milena, but it does
add a simultaneously confusing and revelatory moment when Alex
listens to Milena's phone message, rewinds it, then plays back to
hear a different message which runs longer and sounds less dire. Is it
possible that the film actually leaps inside of Alex's mind as he
recreates the conversation to assure himself he has an alibi? Or is
this detective Netusil's version of the story? When Alex and Netusil
try to re-live the hours following Milena's overdose, Netusil finally
accuses Alex of ''ravishment.'' However, Alex retorts by saying,
''Somehow I get the feeling we are talking about you and not me,''
at which point a door to the outside balcony opens, suggesting a
secret is about to be let out which only an inscrutable eavesdropper
will know. We are pushed further into the ''nothing is what it
seems'' quandary when, in the course of making a routine personality profile, Alex discovers that the man he is investigating is

Milena's husband Stefan. But momentarily, we are led to suspect that Stefan may actually be her father—another of Roeg's attempts to mislead us into thinking we might have missed something.

In *Eureka*, Jack McCann's murder is filmed in the same meticulously evasive manner as Newton's operation. We never know the true killer. We see anonymous hands grabbing a club, a pair of feet shuffling toward a blow torch, Jack's friend Charles Perkins looking guilty as he drops a weapon while leaving the scene before, or maybe after, the murder is committed.

Just before the film's release, Roeg makes a point of adding some extra frames to *Track 29* that reinforce the notion that Linda may be imagining Martin's existence all along. When Linda is at a café panting along to Martin's torrid conversation, we switch to the viewpoint of a waiter who sees Linda talking only to herself.

Roeg's self-enclosed storytelling calls attention to a ruptured communication system. Its gaps tempt us to impose our own meaning. His camera may cut away, or doors may literally shut in our faces, before answers are disclosed, making us frustrated voyeurs with just a fraction of the view. In *"Don't Look Now"*, after Laura boards a boat to the airport on her way back to England, she waits until John is out of sight before turning to some unseen figure; then Roeg abruptly cuts to another scene. Later, when she is at the boarding school, Laura seems oblivious to John's desperate phone call while the Babbages, who run the school, seem intent on keeping us from discovering their own possible part in the shenanigans by shutting the door on us as they escort Laura to her car. There are also the aborted phone calls: the faulty connections the Baxters keep getting between Venice and England; *Bad Timing*'s Milena picking up her receiver to find no answer; the ringing of an unanswered phone when Farnsworth is killed in *The Man Who Fell To Earth*; or in *Eureka* with Tracy and Mayakovsky trying to call Jack when the killers break into his house.

Presented with this myriad of answers always beyond our grasp, we can only feel a mixture of agora- and claustrophobia. This may explain why Roeg likes to indulge in distorted spatial relations: onlookers get the extreme advantage while their objects become even more diminutive. *Walkabout*'s outback is a forbidding place with hostile intruders lurking in the environs. Its seeming expansiveness is, by the film's conclusion, as closed-in as the man-made surroundings. *The Man Who Fell To Earth* supplies a panoramic shot of New Mexico's hillsides, but the grandeur shrinks amid noises of conflicting radio signals (some from earth, others elsewhere) looming over us from the skies. Turner's hideout, Milena's apartment and Jack McCann's estate are also subject to malevolent external forces.

Roeg's interest in the fringe narrative also surfaces in the oblique way he fashions his peripheral characters. They appear as constant curiosities who can elicit more wonder and sympathy than the main figures. We would like to pin down such people as the children's father in *Walkabout* who makes a point of perusing a geology text before killing himself; *Insignificance*'s elevator operator who, like *The Man Who Fell To Earth*'s watcher, may have the missing pieces to the film's riddle as he peers down on America like a bemused zoologist fancying himself at "the center of the Universe." In *Performance*, we notice that Chas's friend Tony removes a painting from his wall after he betrays Chas to the gangsters. When Harry Flowers's gang comes to Tony's house, one of the gangsters shares a flirtation with Tony's wife, perhaps indulging in a mutual secret that could shed some light on the elliptical plot. What should we make of *"Don't Look Now"*'s moody Bishop who surreptitiously strokes Laura's breast when pretending to button his coat and who seems disaffected by what happens to his church? The Venice police chief also seems aware of more than he reveals, as do the various townspeople who look out their windows and close the shutters in fear that John may be looking back at them.

Roeg's peripheral figures also welcome racial paranoia. Roeg seems preoccupied with portraying Peters (the black agent in *The Man Who Fell To Earth*) as the reluctant successor to the white man's corporate nightmare. Inordinate attention is paid to his interracial marriage, especially with a protracted kissing scene between him and his wife tailored to exacerbate the most submerged racial insecurities. *Eureka* is haunted by its sly Haitian servants, one of whom seems to be in some complicity with Claude while another is present during Jack's murder and makes no effort to intervene. *Performance*, especially, is cluttered with references to vigilant black men lurking in the wings: a black garage attendant looking on as Chas and his cronies prepare to ransack an office; the rock musician at the train station who blurts out Turner's address; the photo of

Martin Luther King, Jr. that appears on the wall of the room Chas rents; The Last Poets blaring from Turner's recording studio just before Chas and Turner exchange words for the first time; the boxer in the gymnasium where Tony receives Chas's telephone call; the "black man who drew his knife" in Mick Jagger's "Memo From Turner" song (also a premonition of Altamont)—all designed to draw fuzzy inferences that are inseparable from our own preconceptions and prejudices.

Roeg also provides an infinite regress of perspectives with his visual style. *Performance* employs mirrors and sneaky camera movements; *"Don't Look Now"* and *The Man Who Fell To Earth* use hand-held camera to reinforce a tenuous mood, sometimes following characters from behind or darting into corners to trail some fleeting image. The camera meanders along with John as he wanders through Venice to look for the road leading to the psychic's hotel. When Newton returns to the lake where he had landed and experiences vertigo, the camera moves back and forth among the trees to look for a precipitating cause. The same occurs after Jack finds the gold and looks around the isolated area for someone watching. Also in *Eureka*, just after Claude lures Tracy away from Jack, there is a macabre love scene in which Claude adorns Tracy with a solid gold bikini—all framed by a doorway which makes us feel privy to their intimacy yet distant at the same time. While Martin pursues Linda in *Track 29*, Roeg makes numerous visual allusions to the film *Cape Fear* (about an ex-con seeking to rape and murder his prosecuting attorney's family). The camera is carefully positioned to suggest Linda's proneness to a sexual assault. Periodically, *Track 29* supplies an establishing shot of Linda's home with its menacing satellite dish which seems to monitor her every move.

Bad Timing, however, is the one film which consistently decenters its audience, beginning many scenes with characters partially out of frame, then gradually moving them into mid-shot. We are transformed alternately into the sexual probe's subject and object, our prurient gaze positioned between Milena's legs as we spy with Netusil who watches Alex and Milena's erotic combat. We also become subjects of scrutiny when Roeg begs questions that elicit our private confessions.

Roeg's recurring allusions to Carol Reed's film *The Third Man* also remind us that "we are all being watched." In *The Man Who Fell To Earth*, Newton studies the film on his video screen while trying to convince the doctors that he arrived on earth alone with no witnesses—just as we flash back to the onlooker watching him from atop the hill. *Bad Timing* plays a variation of *The Third Man*'s theme song in the background as Alex questions the mysterious third party about Milena's marriage to Stefan. Alex who, like John Baxter, fails to accurately apply his academic knowledge to his own life, at least comes close to summarizing the fugitive viewpoint's hazards while addressing his classroom. He gives a slide show, starting with the image of a child peeking at his parents during intercourse, signifying nature's "first spy." As the images of Freud, Stalin, J. Edgar Hoover and other "famous spies" appear, he quotes Timothy Leary's dictum from the book *Neuropolitics* that "the guilt-ridden voyeur is usually a political conservative," a statement which anticipates the problems Alex will encounter with Netusil's constant preoccupation with being "normal." Alex, a self-proclaimed liberal, will become more like Netusil—less accepting and more rigid the more he tries to control Milena and the further Netusil tests Alex's emotional security. Alex is a spy being spied on in a city of spies. Like him, we are all vulnerable invaders trying to lure everyone else into our dark room.

MR. ROEG'S DR. JEKYLL

Interview with Allan Scott

SCREENWRITER ALLAN SCOTT IS ROEG'S DIURNAL demon, a godsend for those who wish to see the director tap into an accessible, commercial marketplace, and the bane of those who feel otherwise. Besides co-writing the screenplay for *"Don't Look Now"* (Roeg's most commercially successful venture), Scott has also scripted *Castaway* and is currently planning to write and produce *Cold Heaven*, a future Roeg project based on Brian Moore's novel about a doomed messiah. He is also the screenwriter for Roeg's recent adaptation of Roald Dahl's *The Witches.* Being one of London's wealthiest residents, Scott lives out a patrician existence which is a writer's dream. When his mansion gets too tiresome, he seeks refuge at his villa in the south of France, where he does much of his composition. Scott's devout Roman Catholicism and penchant for conventional genres lend a more traditional slant to Roeg's usual unorthodoxy. During the process of filming *Castaway*, Mr. Scott was particularly interested in making clear that Roeg's career is at a pivotal point in which he will either continue with his daredevil stunts or tidy up his image for straight-laced Hollywood magnates and literal-minded film critics.

* * *

SCOTT: I've never understood the vehemence Nic elicits in critics. He is always accused of pretentiousness, but he is actually the least pretentious person I know. Interestingly enough, I have toyed for some time with telling Roeg to make a commercial masterpiece. He has to shoot it exactly like a commercial. Every so often, he will call me and ask, "Where is my commercial film? Come on!" Finally, I got it. Its number has come up. It is a wonderfully strong straight line story, like *Rocky*. Roeg was actually offered *Rocky* some years ago, and desperately wanted to do it. But Stallone insisted on directing it. It is interesting that he wanted to make that. I think Ryan O'Neal offered it to him.

What would he have done with it?

He would shoot it straight. He would have made it like a commercial picture.

But Roeg likes the anti-hero.

It's strange you should say that because this project I have in mind is about a heroine. He thought of *Rocky* probably because he, at least I think, would rather be a mainstream director than a cult director. And it is only his turn of mind and his passions and fascinations that seem to divert him from that ambition along the way. He wants an audience.

Does he have people advising him on what to do?

Well, he is often offered projects in exchange for which he would have to be a "good boy." Unless he feels in his heart, he can't do it.

And he felt for something like Rocky?

Well, I can't say for sure. It was a screenplay floating around for several years. Who knows what it was like before. It may have had no relationship with the movie we finally saw. There are many other films he wanted to make: *Flash Gordon*, *Out of Africa*. There's *Miraclejack*, the Mayersberg screenplay. He was also going to do *Julia*, with Harold Pinter writing the script.

Roeg says they couldn't make Miraclejack *because it was un-filmable.*

If Nic could call it unfilmable, I can't imagine what it must be. In the last year, we spent a long time together on *Across the River and Into the Trees*. We did three drafts on it. Nic came in on the screenplay that I had already done. We had Kris Kristofferson and Julie Christie. But there was a very adverse reaction, mainly to the ending. The producer liked the previous screenplay better than mine. I just finished, which I am producing as well as having written, *Cold Heaven*, from the book by Brian Moore. It is the next stage on of *"Don't Look Now"*. The story is more explosive. The climax deals with a miraculous appearance, and the logic of the movie is that you have to believe in the reality of it when it comes. The main story is about an illicit love affair. We just did a deal for it. It may be our next.

Roeg prides himself on being very cinematic, but his films have a very strong literary element.

I think that's probably true. Certainly, on any project I've worked on with Nic, his method involves delving into countless literary sources once he has the screenplay intact. He would tell me, ''Read these books and tell me if it gets the scene right.'' One of the books I'm reading now is by Walter De la Mare, called *Desert Island*. It is possible to derive a line of dialogue or there may be a couple of thoughts from such a book. There are other literary references to *Castaway*, like *Robinson Crusoe*, which he looked at very carefully. I gave him a book called *Friday and the Other Island* by Michel Tournier, a wonderful book! Roeg goes through and marks up ideas, and they do end up on the screen. I can recall the scene in *"Don't Look Now"* when the blind woman turns to Donald Sutherland and says, ''Milton loved this city,'' and you think it is just a passing remark. Nic came to us one day and said he thought the psychic needed to say something interesting. So, my partner Chris Bryant and I decided on the Milton reference. For one thing, Milton was also blind. In fact, I have no evidence at all that Milton loved or ever visited Venice. I was trying to come up with something from Milton about his blindness and couldn't, so I gave her that line. Immediately Nic loved the line because it says a whole number of things, doesn't it? Here, the dialogue may be very important because it gives the story more layers. It says something about the woman. Indeed, Donald's blank reaction is also crucial. Nic has a wonderful library, by the way. Like all good directors, he is a great user of other people's ideas. He is steeped in ideas, and is not happy with a project until he has felt his way into what it is all about.

He is full of contradictions: chilly yet able to evoke emotional responses.

That is, of course, what he loves to do more than anything else. To evoke contradictory responses. He is an extraordinarily courageous director, too much for his own good. That whole trial sequence in *Eureka* is something most directors would not have dared! He did it! He knew he was taking the risk. It's wonderful that he's willing to do that.

Tell me more about making Castaway.

You feel your way into a movie. Nic knows he's dealing with the themes he's interested in. As he does this pre-production course, he becomes completely immersed in it. In that process of immersion, he discovers the things he most wants to focus upon. To me, it's a story essentially about how we take what we are with us. Two people go off to the most remote desert island to fulfill a dream and discover that all they've really done is brought their suburb with them.

Are you faithful to Lucy Irvine's book?

Well, neither Roeg nor I are convinced that Irvine told the truth. When we read the book, we thought a very large part of it was speculation. But what is the truth anyway? So, what we tried to do is devise *our* truth. By the time Nic was through with it, it was largely an expression of his thoughts and attitudes. When he envisions a scene, it is never enough. He insists on filling the frame with references. To give you a recent example, I gave Nic a book and asked if he liked it. He loved it, and I had by then acquired the rights. So, then, the first time Nic saw the screenplay, it was a virgin screenplay to him. We then went to California and started to construct the script, and within the first twenty-four hours, Nic realized that there was a whole beat that we were missing. We got out to California to cast the bloody thing and never sent the script out. He was rather startled to discover that even the producer agreed. The purpose of the trip was aborted because, to Nic, the screenplay mattered more. We went through the script page by page. And, in each case, he would be filled with ideas. I essentially acted as filter and stimulator and prompter. So, we came back home, and I wrote the new version, which was final.

Unlike Paul Mayersberg, you tend to shy away from long monologues.

Dialogue isn't all that important to me. People always think that the writer's main contribution is dialogue. Nic is very demanding of writers. He would worry away at a scene endlessly. I'm astonished that he hasn't written his own screenplay. He never writes, he talks, stimulates, challenges. Clearly, his contributions to some of these screenplays are enormous. In my collaborations, he turns the material into the way he sees it. He shoots the script almost exactly. He is one director who actually likes and respects the script.

Does a screenwriter ever give camera directions?

Yes, but not in the sense of using nomenclature. Screenwriters give camera suggestions by the way in which they write. You don't say, "Close-up. Hand grasps doorknob." You just start a fresh paragraph saying, "The gnarled hand turning the doorknob." You would only be interested in camera movement in the sense of atmospherics.

Did you and Roeg work closely on "Don't Look Now"?

Yes we did. I was on hand during much of the filming.

How does he handle something like the love scene between Christie and Sutherland?

Much of it has to do with the amount of trust he can elicit. That's one of the hallmarks of a director. You have to assure actors that you will not show anything that might be thought of as pornographic. Some directors are not that way because you'd know that within days there would be some kind of hot loop out on the street of a similar love scene. I had dinner with someone one night who is on the Board of Film Services, and I believe they showed that love scene. They thought it was made in good taste and judged it as legitimate. I think they even showed it to demonstrate what is acceptable.

Are "Don't Look Now"'s religious and occult references mostly your idea?

That comes from both of us. Religion and faith have always fascinated me. We all have to ask ourselves if we believe in miracles. In *Cold Heaven* also, the story will deal partly with religious phenomena. I like the occult because it has such a potential for drama. It is multi-layered. Organized religion has the same aspects of the occult. When we first talked about *Cold Heaven*, we wanted a miracle in the climax. Audiences are willing to believe in little green men coming down on a Spielberg spacecraft and shaking hands with us; so I must believe they are also willing to believe the hand of God can strike. It must be deeper in our folk myth that God can flick us than the idea of visitors from other planets. Yet, the moment you say to someone you want to do a movie on a religious subject, people think it won't work.

Ken Russell, who is also a devout Catholic, is among the directors Roeg admires. Do you like his religious imagery in The Devils?

Well, it's obsessive. Part of the fascination with religious icons comes with the manner in which they trigger obsessions.

Which direction would you like to see Roeg take? Should he be more daring, or should he straddle a more narrow line and rake in some money, for a change?

I think if I were to criticize anything about his filmmaking, it would be that I don't think he has sufficient interest in the narrative, which I think is what strands audiences. They don't understand why certain things happen at certain times. It is particularly true of *The Man Who Fell To Earth*. I don't think Roeg wants to strand audiences. He wants to bring the viewer with him. I'd like to see him bring in a wider audience. I'm sure he has spoken to you about "stories," dismissing them as mere plot. I don't think you can dismiss mere plot, unless you can be convinced that there is another method of telling a story. I don't think plot underpins what you are doing. I am convinced that Nic is a commercial director. I just don't think he has yet found the project.

"Don't Look Now" has elements of a familiar genre, but there are still moments when he strays.

That and *Walkabout* are his most accessible films. *Insignificance* may also have been, but it dealt with a cerebral subject matter. I would love for Nic to make a conventional genre picture. I know that he worked for some time on *Hammett*. I'd like to see him do a hard-boiled detective story, or a comedy. Anybody who knows him knows he is extremely witty and humorous, with a wonderful breadth of understanding. The thing that is most distinctive to me about him as a person is his incredible breadth of humanity. He is also extraordinarily generous with his time and life. If you can glimpse the personality of the man through the film in the way of Capra, then Nic ought to be making comedies as well. I remember at a press conference in Nice, somebody said he was surprised at what a pleasant fellow Nic was, judging by his movies.

Yet, there's still that sinister side . . .

Well, he really wants to move you in one way or another. He wants a reaction from his audience. It is not that he sets out to do something really sinister. He wants to provoke, to make them see something differently.

THERESA RUSSELL DISGUISED AS KING ZOG FROM *ARIA*

THE NICOLAS ROEG IDENTIKIT

How To Assemble

ROEG: People complained about *Eureka* because they felt the film fell on its ass after Gene Hackman was gone. (*Suddenly lapsing into a James Cagney imitation.*) "After Gene's out of the picture, no one to root for, see?!" But I wanted the film to be about life. One man's life had come to an end. Some of these people at the heads of studios—they don't realize someone like Gene Hackman could be dead in the afternoon and nothing would happen. The painters would still be painting the set. Gene was a maypole, but Tracy is the character that takes over. Tracy *was* Jack McCann in the shell of a woman. And the trial is all about their lives. We see who this person influenced. The lawyer, Mickey Rourke, is wonderful! It's so unusual. People said, "Mickey shouldn't play a lawyer, he's a streetboy!" I said, "Why?" It's rooted in conservatism. You can't shake people out of it.

Having Harvey Keitel play a detective instead of a pimp.

Yes. Well, you know there's another strange story about that. There was one critic who complained about Keitel having an American accent and long hair, that he was just not acting but "posing" as an Austrian detective. We were shooting at a café in

Vienna in the evening. It was a very special café because Hitler used
to go there. People would come from all over the world to see where
he sat and where he took a crap. Anyway, we were shooting, and
there was a minor fire because one of our lamps blew out. So, the fire
engines came, and we had to stop shooting. Then, the Chief of Police
arrived—you will never believe this. He was the double of Harvey.
He had long hair, and he spoke with an American accent. I couldn't
believe it. I got a picture of Harvey with this guy standing next to
him.

Was he smoking also?

He was smoking. He was exactly like him. But critics still say, "It
doesn't matter. He was supposed to be a German who spoke with a
German accent!" I made a point in the film to show that he was
maybe an exchange student in America at one time. Everyone in
Europe speaks English, anyway. Certainly in Austria. They all speak
with American accents. After all, Vienna is a very curious place, a
border town, the only occupied city that was returned to the West by
the Russians. So, the police there are very curious. They are all part
Secret Service people and part policemen.

*There is a Harvard certificate on the detective's wall, which makes
us question his identity all the more.*

Right. The Keitel and Garfunkel characters were the same man.
They dressed the same, moved the same. They may have connected,
but it was too late when Milena's husband barged in to say she was
alive. So, the detective couldn't just write Linden off as another
solved police file. That's the only thing anyone can do in life, just
give the facts. Facts are only something you tell a policeman.

What good are facts unless you can distort them?

Absolutely. Look at the policeman in *"Don't Look Now"*. When
he shows Julie Christie the Identikit, he asks, "Is this the woman?"
and she answers, "Yes, but she didn't look like that." Then he
says, "It doesn't matter." It's bizarre. The police put out these
Identikits of people, but if that Identikit ever walked into a room,
he'd look like Frankenstein's monster.

How about the fun you have with sexual identity?

It's certainly in *Performance*. Probably more so in *Eureka*. Tracy becomes an extension of her father in the guise of a female. The gender is not that important, it's just the shell. Paul and I wanted to convey their closeness, and that's when we came upon the idea of the dinner party where they exhibit their mutual gift for mathematics. I think I like androgyny—when the sexes get mixed up. While I was shooting *Bad Timing*, Art Garfunkel came up to me and said he realized he was really playing me. But I told him that he was only part of it. I challenged him to decipher when I was wearing the trousers and when I was wearing the dress.

* * *

THE RULES TO THE NICOLAS ROEG IDENTIKIT ARE AS bendable as the identities. The following points are just suggestions to assist you in your own "mix or match" strategies.

RULE 1: *DOPPELGÄNGERS*

Roeg never creates a *single* character. There are instead character *clusters* which often appear as Doppelgängers, mirror images or foils. Just take two or more characters within a film, or even between films, to discover similarities of physique, personality, clothing styles, mannerisms, vocal intonations, as well as surface disparities that reveal deeper likenesses.

The obvious doublings:

Chas and Turner in *Performance* begin by seeming at opposite poles, but, in the end, merge as a composite person driving to their execution in the gangster limousine.

In *The Man Who Fell To Earth*, Newton and Dr. Bryce assume a Christ-Judas relationship. Both abandon their families and even end up sharing the same bed partner. But their rivalry surfaces when it comes time for the ultimate showdown. When Bryce visits Newton's desert hideaway to hear the alien admit his true identity, he is like the prototypical gunslinger about to draw fire on the stranger in town.

Bad Timing continues this enmity-love struggle. Alex Linden and Detective Frederich Netusil dress and smoke with the same affectations. They are also of similar size and stature (which are likewise similar to Roeg's). Only their contrasting occupations separate them, and even this demarcation vanishes when they later engage in an inadvertent job switch. Alex goes about town to investigate Milena's history while Frederich grows more intrigued by Alex and Milena's psychosexual imbroglio. While trying to pry the truth about the alleged "ravishment" out of Alex, Frederich appropriates the psychoanalyst's role into his police science when he finally admits, "What is detection if not confession?"

Then, there are the *less* obvious pairs:

People as diametrically opposed as The Professor and The Senator in *Insignificance* are equally enmeshed in private ethical dilemmas and play parallel roles in events leading to the Cold War. In *Performance*, Turner transforms into Harry Flowers and becomes Chas's new puppeteer in the hallucinatory "Memo From Turner" sequence, abandoning the Dandy image for a ruffian, greaser appearance.

RULE 2: *INTERMEDIATE PERSONAE*

As Roeg's dramas get more complex, the interrelationships and metaphorical cross-references between characters get more specialized until the pairs splinter off into groups.

In *Eureka*, Jack McCann and his supposedly close friend Charles Perkins are in psychic pursuit of each other. After witnessing Jack burn his fingers on the magic stone, Charles later emerges from the wings to examine the rock as it turns cold again at his touch. The moment Jack's fingers get singed, Roeg cuts to son-in-law Claude deflowering Tracy—an implied connection between the three men that fructifies on the night of Jack's death with Claude and Charles as the prime murder suspects. Just as the killers break into McCann's house, Roeg slips in what appears to be a quick shot of Jack and Charles standing together one last time before a mirror. But Claude soon usurps Charles's place as Jack's double at the very end when, before forsaking Tracy to sail alone into the sunrise, he gazes at his reflection to utter, "I knew it would be you"—the last words Jack cries as Claude enters the room to witness, or maybe even abet, Jack's slaughter. Are Claude's final words a manifestation of guilt? Or do they indicate that he is actually the apparition in Frieda's prophecy at the beginning, as she proclaims that, when the war ends, another will succeed Jack's quest for self-knowledge?

Sometimes Roeg implies connections between people by exaggerating their physical differences. Who can forget the precious scene in *Castaway* when a scruffy, bearded Gerald (already looking the part of Robinson Crusoe) studies a storefront terrarium of his primitive paradise only to encounter a bald and immaculate entrepreneur gazing back at him from the other side of the glass? In *Eureka*, Roeg makes Mayakovsky and his daughter Ester morphological antitheses—perhaps suggesting that the gangster lacks the affinity with his own offspring that Jack enjoys with Tracy.

Roeg may insinuate character mergers by matching poses or capturing people through identical camera movements. In *Walkabout*, an indirect link between the aborigine and the children's father occurs with the shot of the dying ox (with which the aborigine identifies) filmed through the same loop as the father falling back against the burning car after he shoots himself. Notice also the killer dwarf's stabbing motion in *"Don't Look Now"* reflect daughter Christine's gestures when she plays by the pond. Roeg suggests, in *The Man Who Fell To Earth*, that Oliver Farnsworth and Mr. Peters are at opposite ends of America's corporate evolution when dissolving Farnsworth's feeble body being thrown out of a skyscraper with Peters jumping into his swimming pool after ordering Farnsworth's liquidation.

However, the most interesting parallels occur in *Eureka*. Jack's early concubine Frieda and his wife Helen are shown in similar reclining postures on a sofa: Frieda, when she laments over Jack's failure as a lover, and Helen, after learning of her husband's murder. Claude, while mourning over his mother's death, puts his head against a couch whose design resembles the blood-stained bedsheet on which Jack is later decapitated. The stealthy camera movement onto Jack's bewildered expression when Frieda describes the gold he will soon discover recurs on Claude's face at the trial when he describes Jack's mutilated corpse.

RULE 3: *INDISTINCT PHYSIOGNOMIES*

Roeg also melts people into each other's facial geometries. In *Performance*, when Turner and Pherber rearrange his image with a mustache and bowler hat for a fake passport photo, Chas resembles the lawyer in the first part of the film who tries to prosecute the mob. A Magritte painting, later delivered to Turner's house by a pair of identical twins, contains a face which looks a great deal like the lawyer's client.

Alex, in *Bad Timing*, hallucinates facial similarities when combing the streets of Vienna to find the man who matches the one in the photograph he thinks is Milena's boyfriend. In *"Don't Look Now"*, John Baxter, for a moment, thinks that the body dredged from a canal might be Laura, when it is actually another of the faceless homicide victims that even Venice's police chief fails to identify. Amid *"Don't Look Now"*'s ongoing "who's who?" teasers, we are reminded that Laura also resembles one of the sisters' daughters. Later, when John reports his wife as a missing person, the police present a composite drawing of one of the sisters which looks more like the hotel proprietor. Even as he listens to John recount his misfortunes, the police chief traces over the same drawing until it resembles the killer's face which flashes at the climax. Perhaps the only person in the film who can truly distinguish features is ironically the blind woman, who relies on touch rather than sight and even keeps a bust of one of her relatives among an assortment of family photographs.

Toward *The Man Who Fell To Earth*'s conclusion, Bryce ages about twenty years and looks almost exactly like Newton's mysterious witness who (also resembling one of Farnsworth's killers) returns to the alien's bedside the night before the internment ends. Even Newton and Mary-Lou seem less as lovers and more as extensions of each other as a side-by-side close-up of their faces reveals identical beauty marks. Then, in *Track 29*, the truck driver who drives in and out of the narrative (and bears some resemblance to Martin) may be Linda's rapist or even a chimera of Martin's future self. A café waiter (also resembling the truck driver) is the only character who notices that Linda is hallucinating Martin's existence all along.

RULE 4: *THE BOOTSTRAP APPROACH*

Roeg often prefers to have people collide with each other several places at one time.

Newton's teleported image, which haunts Bryce on the evening before their first formal encounter, is just as inexplicable as the moment in *"Don't Look Now"* when the Bishop suddenly rises from his sleep seconds before John Baxter's attack; or in *Eureka* when Tracy grasps her neck the moment her father is killed.

Even Roeg's original conception for *Performance*'s ending attempts to amalgamate physical and psychic boundaries. Instead of the present version in which Chas rides away to his death in the gangster limo, Roeg wanted the car to re-emerge out of New York's Holland Tunnel, implying that the sort of identity exchange between Turner and the gangsters is occurring everywhere.

The same idea can also be conveyed through a mediating object that unites persons. *Walkabout* intercuts the children playing on a barren tree with another tree holding the father's rotting body, another juxtaposition which prepares us for the aborigine's death.

One instance in *Bad Timing* cross-cuts Alex and Frederich in their respective homes: Alex mounts the same picture of a maze which Frederich takes down from his wall. Roeg himself claims that he added this brief interlude to suggest that Alex is entering the quandary to which Frederich has grown all too accustomed. But the moment Frederich throws his coat on the bed where Alex's supposed necrophile orgy takes place, he and Alex merge as both Milena's as well as each others' psychic rapists.

RULE 5: *BLURRING SUBJECT AND OBJECT*

Roeg often employs an anthropomorphism theme, letting characters merge with their inanimate surroundings.

The aborigine in *Walkabout* commits suicide when he identifies with the external environment he is supposed to subdue. In *Castaway*, the idea that the island is actually Lucy's new lover surfaces when the natural rock formations resemble a human body. In one instance, Roeg switches the telephoto lens to a huge mound in the distance which looks like the fist Gerald makes in one of his many frustration fits.

At other times, characters become mere symbols of the places they inhabit. The people in *The Man Who Fell To Earth* and *Bad Timing* thrive in border towns, torn between conflicting worlds. When Alex finds his life hopelessly jumbled, he whines to Milena that ''to be in between is to be no place at all.'' Later when Alex and Milena confront each other at a university campus, the camera pans back and forth between their faces until the blurred background separating them dominates the scene—just as the river becomes the film's final image, no longer obscured by the human activity on the bridge.

RULE 6: *IDENTITY CONFUSION AND SEXUAL AMBIGUITY*

Many of Roeg's identity struggles can be reduced to a sexual combat between masculine forces that impose distinctions and feminine powers that erode them. This often involves androgynous character transformations wherein the male, sometimes resisting till the bitter end, appropriates female characteristics.

In *Performance*, our first introduction to Turner's ambisexual universe occurs during a *ménage à trois* between Lucy, Pherber and himself, filmed through tinted filters and vacillating camera speeds which make the bodies indistinguishable. Pherber later assaults Chas's machismo by dressing him in elaborate costumes with make-up and powders to bring out his "female feel." This prepares us for the consummate sex scene when, through the magic of devious editing, Chas alternately makes love to Turner and Lucy, who are fashioned to look alike.

Chas's girlfriend Donna (who identifies herself in the opening segment as the "cabaret artiste" for which Turner initially mistakes Chas) is the first of several personages staging Chas's transformation. She leaves scratches on his back that correspond to the whip wounds his ex-boyfriend Joey later inflicts. Even Chas's gangster cronies comprise a homoerotic cabal that taunts him into admitting his sexual past. When Joey and his thugs thrust Chas into a kinky rumble, we see various incriminating artifacts littered throughout the apartment: a portrait of a female who looms like his dreaded alter-ego, photos of Chas and Harry Flowers in sexual congress, the word "poof" (a misspelled British slang term for "faggot") splashes across the wall like a blood smear.

As the female influences dominate, the men waver. "Isn't it strange how the sexes age differently?" the police chief in *"Don't Look Now"* reflects while peering out at two women on the street who resemble the sisters. "Men seem to grow more distinct while women seem to merge." His lackadaisical attitude contrasts sharply with *Bad Timing*'s detective Netusil who describes women as "a moral and physical sewer'' who ''envy our strength, our ability to master reality.''

In some cases, Roeg's characters are just stages away from becoming their opposite gender. This makes Roeg one of the greatest practitioners of understated drag in film history. The first time Alex and Milena meet at a party, Alex plays at being demure (and even wears a trace of mascara) while Milena plays the aggressor. In *Castaway*, Gerald applies Lucy's eye shadow before exerting his waning valor by trying to force Lucy to have sex. Like Chas in *Performance*, who gradually transforms from gangster to tart, *Eureka*'s Jack McCann starts off as a hardy prospector but ends up looking more like a hapless dowager in a flowing caftan while his wife browbeats him. *Eureka*'s entire theme is predicated on Tracy taking over Jack's soul, making the characteristically feminine subject of love and romance eclipse any escapist male adventure.

Just as he reverses history and gender by casting a female for King Zog in his *Aria* segment, Roeg likes to feminize male heroics. In *Eureka*, on the night of Jack's murder, Tracy symbolically takes over as the new family head by donning a masculine riding outfit while husband Claude gets swooned away in an erotic voodoo snake dance with an androgynous male Haitian. This prepares them for the ordeal in the courtroom when Tracy psychologically emasculates Claude in order to acquit him.

RULE 7: *EVEN THE BOUNDARIES TO EACH FILM ARE INDEFINITE*

Characters and images permutate from movie to movie.

For example: The Indian in *Insignificance* and Newton in *The Man Who Fell To Earth* are both detached prophets, of sorts, fixated on Manhattan's skyline and doomed to endure tortuous elevator rides. The swamp water Newton sips when he arrives on earth looks much like the putrid concoction Gerald offers Lucy in *Castaway* to consecrate their new life on Tuin. Likewise, Martin, *Track 29*'s British miscreant, arrives in a small North Carolina town with the same hair color and sense of dislocation as Newton when he arrives in Haneyville.

During his captivity, Newton watches Carol Reed's *The Third Man*, whose images stick in his mind when, at the very end, we find him sulking at an outdoor café, posing with a wide-brimmed hat and

coat hanging over his shoulders, identical to Reed's Holly Martins
character (Joseph Cotton) just before he betrays his racketeer friend
Harry Lyme (Orson Welles). But while Newton acquires the
traitor's demeanor, Bryce, the real traitor, finally tracks him down
to engage in a demented reminiscence. Once again, Roeg switches
the identities, obliquely suggesting that Newton is maybe guilty of
self-betrayal. When the very last credit goes up and the camera drops
slightly, we see all that is left to Newton are the hat, coat and chair,
with no body.

Roeg's taste for sexual ambiguity dates as far back as *Fahrenheit
451* when Montag, the fireman, foreshadows Chas, with his
regimented and conservative lifestyle until he falls in love with Linda
(a tomboy figure whom *Performance*'s Lucy resembles). Montag's
sense of self crumbles the more she exerts her influence. By the
film's conclusion, when Linda has turned his mind around completely, there is a lap dissolve between his face and hers, similar to
Performance's lap dissolve between Chas and Turner. Also, when a
police bulletin is issued for Montag's arrest, multiple images of the
back of Montag's head fill several television screens—a visual
association that will recur in *Performance* and *The Man Who Fell
To Earth*.

We also cannot forget *Performance*'s lawyer who, while defending
business "mergers," watches his jury dissolve into the audience at
a porno film. The lawyer's words echo in *The Man Who Fell To
Earth* when a septuagenarian official orders Newton's corporation
destroyed in order that we may impose a global "modern
America." In turn, *Eureka*'s Mayakovsky reduces the entire
world's identity to "Americans who speak different languages."

Of course, in these endless variations on the struggle to know and
simultaneously deny who we are, Roeg obviously infuses his own
variegated identity into the subject matter. He could be perpetrating
his hagiography by having the Bishop in *"Don't Look Now"* mention that the church John restores is in memory of St. Nicholas.
Roeg may also be implying his incrimination by adorning the
homicidal dwarf with a red hood to suggest Santa Claus. But,
perhaps this man/woman demon is not really Roeg at all but, instead, another of his many nemeses who (vaguely resembling a
famous American movie critic) seethes from the other side of the
mirror.

MASTERS OF MISDIRECTION

The Wedding of Nicolas Roeg and Edward D. Wood, Jr.

ROEG: Director? Perhaps it's a nice name for a job. It sounds like an executive bossing people around, but there is ultimately not too much direction. The best you can be is a kind of jockey. Look at this table we're sitting on, for instance. This is how we are, the objects placed at random. Somebody in a film crew would say, ''Move that ashtray! It's in front of his fingers.'' So what? That's the way it is! What is a ''better'' frame? What painter goes to a landscape, looks at a beautiful mountain with hills and trees, and then shifts over? Every view is a view. It's very difficult to get that random factor. I try and let it happen. Even if a rose is stuck up somebody's nose, that's where it is, it's what I'm looking at. It's very odd how people love interfering with things.

It's easy to feel cheated if a movie looks too good.

It's very difficult to define what's bad or good, anyway. I prefer something clumsy to something artificial. Some of the most interesting things happen when you leave them up to chance. Imperfection can be so perfect. This happened in *''Don't Look Now''* with the man playing the Inspector. He couldn't speak a word of English. I'd never before come across anyone who didn't even know how to say "yes" or even "the." It was like hearing blindness! They said they'd get an interpreter who could coach him, but I said, "No, I don't want any coach." All I wanted to do was explain the scene to him, not tell him what the words meant. I wanted him to parrot the words. So, the first shot was Donald Sutherland coming down the corridor, looking for the Inspector's office. We lined up the camera, tracking him down. While we were shooting over his shoulder, he knocked on the door. But the cameraman forgot to line up the shot properly. When the Inspector says, "Come in," we pan, open the door, but discover this desk lamp blocking his head. The operator was about to yell "Cut!" but I motioned for him to leave the scene alone. It was perfect. In that big office, the Inspector has to move his head from behind a tiny lamp.

That was a mistake?

Fantastic, isn't it? You could never have done that artificially. Neither he nor Sutherland knew what the fuck was going on. That set the scene's tone.

In Eureka, *once you set Theresa Russell up in the courtroom, you put her in probably one of the most awkward positions any performer could possibly assume.*

It had to be done that way, though. She was trying to bring out the truth about herself and her husband. When you get that close to the truth, you are always in an awkward position. I wanted that vulnerability. It's tragic that people took that trial scene so literally. If you take it to be literal or realistic, it's lunacy. The lights don't go down in a real courtroom, nor would people be allowed to shout at each other like that. They were putting *themselves* on trial, and she saved his neck by destroying him. They both risked their egos; so I ended up filming the situation in a risky manner, I guess. The public just ridiculed the whole movie, that scene especially, to shreds. Perhaps I failed, or perhaps in twenty years time it will be better appreciated. It all depends on one's viewpoint, whether something is brilliant or abysmal.

* * *

NICOLAS ROEG'S FILMS AND PHILOSOPHY ARE SO RIFE
with contradictions that he would not be surprised nor annoyed to
find himself (one of the most technically proficient directors) converging in a warped continuum with Edward D. Wood, Jr. (the most
technically inept). Egregious as it may seem, the comparison is
unavoidable. No other two directors have so ingeniously mastered
the art of ambivalent intention by refusing to reveal whether we are
really laughing at *them* or they at *us*.

On the one hand, we have Wood, considered by some as Hollywood's village idiot, an eccentric whose films are notorious for their
abysmal acting, inane scripts, slack plots and chintzy set designs.
Spoon-fed on slick productions, most viewers (especially the post-
Spielberg circuit) may approach a Wood film with condescension,
fancying they share a joke at the director's expense. This is until
they are disarmed by those brilliant moments, such as *Glen or
Glenda's* hallucination sequences, Tor Johnson's ceremonious ascent from the grave in *Plan Nine From Outer Space,* or the laboratory catastrophe in *Bride of the Monster*—all of which contain
enough obvious camp and surprising visual acuity to make us
wonder if we may have either underestimated Wood or over-
estimated our sophistication. How are we supposed to interpret the
religious sermon at the conclusion of *The Violent Years* (the
juvenile delinquency melodrama which Wood had scripted) that is
too ponderous and corny to be believed, or *Bride of the Monster*,
when the woman the evil doctor hypnotizes for his experiment
enters the laboratory wearing a full bridal gown, which the doctor's
deformed assistant proceeds to fondle?

Roeg's situation is, of course, more devious. With good financial
backing, photographic expertise, and first-rate actors, he manages to
recapture Wood's ironic spirit. Roeg counterpoints his otherwise
high quality productions with intermittent plot discrepancies,
awkward dialogue and other delightfully maladroit techniques that
provide a unique tension. *The Man Who Fell To Earth* is as stunning as the greatest sci-fi films, yet it flounders at just the right
moments with elliptical time spans and hysterical editing. Likewise,
Eureka's uneven pacing and fuzzy distinctions between real and surreal make it look as if it is made by at least two distinctively different
directors. But what would be written off as an unforgivable *faux pas*
for most auteurs becomes Roeg's stylistic virtue.

We may get a better idea of the Roeg-Wood merger by examining some of their mutual strategies, the most apparent being their tenuous dramatics. Consider the overwrought monologues of Bela Lugosi in *Bride of the Monster* and Helena Kallioniotes in *Eureka*. Both scenes are pushed beyond tolerable limits. At the same time, we stay mesmerized by the actors' ability to arouse contrary emotions with single gestures.

Possibly intuiting that this would be his last speaking part, Lugosi, as the mad Dr. Vornoff, presents one of celluloid's most exaggerated and paranoid performances. Intent on creating a race of atomic super-beings, Vornoff must convince a rival not to sabotage his operation: "I have no home. Hunted, despised, living like an animal. The jungle is my home. I will show the world that I can be its master. I will perfect my own race of people . . . which will conquer the world!" All the while Lugosi speaks, the camera mercilessly stays on his contorted face, making us wait for some muscular twitch or other form of comic relief to mitigate the situation that is embarrassing for Wood, Lugosi, but mostly for ourselves who, duped into watching it, cannot decide whether to be nauseated or moved. Suddenly, we suspect that the director has an over-reaching and overbearing intelligence that we are too smug to grasp.

The same occurs in *Eureka* when Kallioniotes, who plays Frieda the Gypsy, laments to Jack McCann about their failed romance. Suggesting both Camille and Vampira, she strikes a meretricious pose on her sofa and lapses into a somnolent tirade: "For you the gold was everything. You'd never give up. We had a crock of gold between us. His cock and my crack, a crock of gold! It was more than love, it was a power. Then, one day I looked out, the sun was shining, it was spring, and Jack was dead." Like Wood, Roeg uses unsettling close-ups, but he also performs visual gyrations around Frieda to make the scene even more absurd. He essentially turns the camera into a magnifying lens that threatens to reveal a slight speck of self-parody in the melodrama.

Roeg and Wood indulge in enough exaggerated bathos to produce a warped realism and honesty, making the actors ham it up during the most intense or touching moments. In *Plan Nine From Outer Space,* one of the aliens sounds like a used car dealer when he tries to explain to the dense earthlings why their nuclear madness must be squelched. In *Night of the Ghouls,* the most laughable acting comes out of an elderly couple emerging from a police station after finding out their daughter is killed. But the best example is Wood's masterpiece *Glen or Glenda*—a potent social drama about transvestism. Wood, himself a transvestite, adds a macabre tinge to this otherwise ham-handed appeal for societal tolerance. An earnest conversation between a police chief and a psychiatrist about the plight of cross-dressers is intercut with such surrealistic excesses as Lugosi satirizing all of his past horror performances or a bound woman being raped by Satan. Then, what is supposed to be the most human scene of all becomes the silliest: Glen's girlfriend, upon learning of her boyfriend's fetish, shows her acceptance by rising from her chair (a musical crescendo accompanying) to hand him her angora sweater.

The drama is no less poignant or ludicrous in *Eureka* when Tracy tries to protect her husband Claude from her father Jack's violent reprisals. Holding Claude in her arms while Jack wields a hatchet over both of them, Tracy tries to explain why love conquers all: "I don't want your gold. I want flesh. I want to kiss human flesh. I want to touch it, I want to fuck it. . . ," at which point she licks the blood from her wounded shoulder. Also in *"Don't Look Now"*, during a crucial moment when John confronts Laura about her faltering mental health, he tries to destroy any illusions she may have about contacting their dead daughter: "Laura, our daughter is dead. She does not come with messages from beyond the fucking grave. Our daughter is dead. Dead, Dead, Dead, Dead, Dead!" Here, the camera is misplaced and intrusive, as if we are an uninvited third party muscling in on an all-too-intimate situation. In *Bad Timing*, Harvey Keitel's Detective Netusil almost corners Alex Linden into admitting he had raped Milena Vodnik. But, as he repeats the word "ravishment" several times, Keitel's portrayal invites chuckles at the least appropriate moments. Once again, our consternation and sympathies are ignited simultaneously as human interactions are de-sensitized by under- and over-statement.

Roeg and Wood are also able to turn narrative discontinuity into an innovation. *Plan Nine From Outer Space* and *The Man Who Fell To Earth* derive their strength from shaky premises. The aliens in Wood's film already undertake their project to bring dead earthlings back to life at the beginning, making much of the remaining story seem redundant. Roeg likewise keeps his alien's mission open-ended. Newton starts his elaborate plans to return to his planet as

soon as he lands—the exact purpose for the visit never made completely clear. The fact that Newton acquires his fortune by selling
gold rings for twenty dollars each certainly does not help in lending
credibility to the script. Both directors also specialize in wedging incomprehensible subplots into their stories to throw us off and to suggest deeper meanings precisely because they seem so superfluous.
The generic crime yarn in *Jailbait* (Wood's salute to *film noir*) is
suddenly interrupted by an insufferable nightclub routine with a
comedian in black face. *Glen or Glenda*, for no apparent reason,
lapses into fifties-style pornography. *"Don't Look Now"*'s extended love scene and *Eureka*'s voodoo sequence have also prompted
critics to question any integral purpose.

Wood, who is not alive to either defend or indict himself, remains
an ongoing mystery. Roeg, however, from various interviews, admits that he likes to put his actors in positions where they must
either sink, swim or preferably both. He casts a star like Bernie
Casey (known mostly for his athletic and black tough roles) as a
government agent who, outnumbered by a team of white geezer
politicians, struggles with his lines. Besides revealing supposed flaws
in the performance and script, such scenes suggest that this is the
way anyone would appear in similar alien surroundings. Bowie's
problematic acting in the beginning of *The Man Who Fell To Earth*,
when he meets his lawyer Farnsworth, is also strained and gangly
enough to fit the story's awkward situation. Keitel's gauche role as a
Vienna detective (it is impossible to figure out which accent he is
trying to adopt) is also consistent with *Bad Timing*'s personality
deception theme. The same lack of verisimilitude applies to *Eureka*
when Roeg invites trouble by casting Mickey Rourke as an Italian,
Joe Pesce as a Jew and Rutger Hauer as a Frenchman.

Roeg's penchant for deliberate miscasting dates back to his work
with Truffaut on *Fahrenheit 451*. Oskar Werner (who plays the
main character, Montag) is blatantly ill-equipped for the part,
especially when he laboriously recites his lines with a thick German
accent while everyone else in the story is British. Roeg provides a
ticklish anecdote about how Truffaut reveled over Werner's inept
demeanor and flagging enthusiasm. In the scenes where Werner was
supposed to be emotional, Truffaut asked him to think the opposite
of what he was supposed to feel, even making him visualize a rubber
duck whenever a scene required him to be serious. Truffaut also

divorced the film's script of any idiomatic familiarities by having it initially written in French, translated into English, translated back into French, and then into English again. This results in a flat verbal exchange tedious for some viewers but perhaps fitting for an over-surveyed population deprived of written words. In parts, Truffaut even uses a double for Werner, which explains the varying hair lengths which could either be a lame oversight or a subtle way to convey that Montag is essentially two different men. This also complements Christie's dual role as Montag's wife and girlfriend.

Roeg continues these disparities in his main work by exploiting natural language barriers. With *Performance*, Michele Breton (who plays Lucy) knows no English and takes a two-week crash course. James Fox also has to wall himself up in a hotel to practice a cockney accent, and he still occasionally slips out of character. Add this to Mick Jagger's lackadaisical and pseudo-aristocratic enunciations, and we have a verbal cacophony that reinforces *Performance*'s theme of warring identities. *Walkabout*'s David Gumpilil (the aborigine) also knows no English, adding the essential handicap to strengthen the film's alienation mood. By the time Theresa Russell slurs in and out of her southern drawl in *Track 29*, we know that consistency is the hobgoblin of myopic movie-goers.

In this Midnight Movie era, Roeg and Wood's talents are mistakenly credited to others as well. A film like Ken Hughes's *Sextette* belabors the excruciating dissonance between Mae West's self-aggrandizement and everyone else's derision, but not for a moment can anyone believe it is anything but a joke (except for West, and she's dead). There are also directors like Herschell Gordon Lewis, whom Roeg commemorates in *The Man Who Fell To Earth* when Candy Clark responds to David Bowie's Grade B alien suit with a Grade B scream. But Lewis, whose movies cater to a well-defined drive-in cult crowd, manufactures trash in exchange for cash and never purports to do otherwise. There is also Ken Russell who sweetens his more solemn subjects with crumbs of low comedy, but usually elicits the audience's canned laughter at the calculated moments without begging questions. Neither Roeg nor Wood would let us off so easily.

Roeg's closest link to Wood thus far is *Eureka*'s now historical trial scene. Jack McCann has been murdered, and Tracy's husband Claude is on trial as the culprit. After numerous testimonies, Claude finally calls Tracy to the witness stand to defend him. What begins as a prosaic courtroom episode transforms into one of the most absurd, intriguing, tendentious, and brilliant interludes ever filmed. The lights dim until only Claude and Tracy are spotlighted. Tracy then delivers a lengthy descant on the metaphysics of ''true love'' and, with Charles Manson logic, equates Claude's lack of passion with his inability to kill. ''You may have come close to murder, but you didn't do it . . . If only you'd been a man of God. If only you'd been an artist. You fell into life, Claude! You stumbled and tripped, but I picked you up. You think it was *you* who seduced *me?* It was only desire . . . You couldn't kill Jack McCann. You'll never kill anybody . . .''

As Theresa Russell whimpers and hyperventilates, the camera stays on her face, only intermittently recording the placid spectators. Still, we do not know whether what transpires is reality or dream. Certainly *Eureka*'s entire look has the same malarial charm as the notorious Edgar Allan Poe essay from which Roeg borrows the inspiration and title. In a fevered attempt to describe the order of the universe, Poe imbues his own *Eureka* with meandering prose and spasmodic bursts of insight, as if aware that this would be his final piece before death. Roeg, as well, makes a film about ecstasy and madness and becomes the very thing he is shooting.

We can conclude that Roeg and Wood are unique species who assure us that there is life beyond camp and that the four sides of a movie's frame are an illusory border. Both wreak revenge on their constricting medium by making their obsessions interfere with the filmmaking process, deploying a suicidal approach that ironically lends a strange vitality most other films lack. If we can call what Roeg and Wood do errors, then no two directors make more interesting mistakes. If these errors are intended, then none can so deftly lay bare the device only to mystify it once more.

THE TRIALS OF THERESA RUSSELL

IF EVER BLESSED WITH THE ODD FORTUNE TO ENTER Mr. Roeg's house, prepare to be led up the stairs and into his study where, among countless books and movie paraphernalia, you will encounter a bust of Theresa Russell's head (used for *Insignificance*'s holocaust sequence) leering from one of his book cases. In many respects, this disconcerting artifact says it all. Theresa Russell, whether alive or inanimate, is an everpresent phantom who continues to loom over the director's life and oeuvre.

For Roeg, Russell is an object of compassion, adulation, derision and self-exploration. This is what makes their relationship more interesting than the standard director-actress "arrangement." By using her in almost all of his latter films, he not only gives his wife a job or flaunts her as an acquisition but puts *himself* in front of the camera. Roeg has even admitted that, in *Bad Timing* especially, Russell's characters are just as much a part of his personality as the male figures.

Theresa Russell's performances, in fact, defy all Hollywood moguls to pigeonhole her as they have other actresses of her ilk. This is perhaps because Roeg subjects her to some of the most challenging, enervating and often embarrassing roles. Whether fucking Art Garfunkel on a staircase, wailing incessantly in a courtroom about the philosophical amalgam of ''true love'' and ''murder,'' getting mutilated in a nuclear explosion, or dodging an assassin's bullets while masquerading as the King of Albania, Ms. Russell, guided by her crazed mentor, goes into avenues which few actresses, or actors for that matter, have dared to venture.

The day that I meet her, Russell is in a domestic muddle, trying to organize her son Stanton's birthday party while contending with a tribe of neighborhood imps slobbering over the Roegs' cherished coffee table which bears an inscription of the Robert Service poem from *Eureka*. Father Nicolas is also on hand, temporarily neutralizing his director's aura in order to grapple with the instructions for operating an instamatic camera. It seems that Roeg views the occasion as an all-too-familiar connubial routine while Russell, a freshly consecrated mother, is more outwardly enthused.

Connubiality (its degradations more than its joys) is the subject matter that Roeg and Russell seem to indulge in most these days. Hailed as ''the High Priestess of Doom'' by some critics, Russell represents a radical change occurring in Roeg's career when, following *The Man Who Fell To Earth*, he begins to pay *exclusive* attention to the dynamics of human relationships, especially those in which husband and wife are less complementary opposites and more like personality rivals. With Russell, a certain combination of realism and twisted romance enters Roeg's work. In films like *Bad Timing*, *Eureka*, *Insignificance* and *Track 29*, we see heavy-handed allusions to a private domestic battlefront whose melodrama and slapstick never stop. In some ways, she also guides Roeg along a more neo-conservative route. Even *Bad Timing*, as risqué as it is, suggests an apotheosis of the missionary position that *Castaway* (the first film without Russell in five years) confirms. After *Bad Timing*, the angst and sexual confusion of the seventies make way for wedding cake copulation. *Eureka* alternates from a mythology of warriors and Rhinemaidens to a soap opera spat. *Insignificance* offers nostalgic glimpses into an earlier Hollywood's regimented boy-girl roles. When asked about the parochial nature of these later films, especially *Castaway*, compared to films like *Performance* and *The Man Who Fell To Earth*, Russell sounds reactionary: ''The most important relationships are between male and female, aren't they?''

But despite her protests, Russell embodies Roeg's ongoing

fascination with gender ambiguity as she exhibits everything seductive in males as well as females. She can at one point be so sultry and demure; then suddenly exert a masculine brashness that makes the male lead diminutive by comparison. Even her role as the murderess in Bob Rafelson's *Black Widow* is laced with enough of the brooding dominatrix to prepare us for a hinted but unrealized love affair between her character and Debra Winger's. Russell may defend her spouse's recent fixation on heterosexual duets (in their conventional trappings) by maintaining it is all part of his regard for ''nature and the origins of life,'' even though every Roeg part she has played thus far involves someone either unable or refusing to have a child. Regardless of Roeg's purported nature theories, it is obvious that *everyone* in his stories, no matter how fertile they are, succumbs to Malthusian hell in reverse.

At times, Roeg seems to consign his wife to existential limbo, adorning her with all of the hackneyed pagan relics of a fecund goddess, yet pitting her against a Judeo-Christian ethos which stifles her hedonism as she genuflects to patriarchal authority. When Roeg looks into the mirror at Russell, what does he see? Wife? Mother? Actress? Whore? Virgin? Hermaphrodite? Wetnurse? Hood ornament? Or are both he and she keeping vigilance for some other more resilient and untamable animal fighting to escape *all* social codes or preordained biological roles?

After talking with Ms. Russell, we get the impression that her relationship with the director does not merit so many nosy, gossipy speculations. ''Of course, we are very much involved with one another, and I love him deeply; but ultimately, I'm just an actress.'' Indeed, she is very shy, unassuming and downright unfriendly to personal questions about her marriage, perhaps defensive about being in a situation which invites so many glib, though unavoidable, Freudian clichés. She echoes the words of her character Tracy in *Eureka* who, while being interrogated by her husband in a courtroom, retorts that ''a marriage is two people, and they are the only two people who can really understand it.''

Notwithstanding her resolve at separating the actress identity from the rest of her life, Russell, like Roeg, never fails to betray duplicitous motives. In recalling some of her most intense scenes, she invariably makes allusions to her off-screen politics. ''Nic and I are really soul-mates more than just husband and wife. Every time we do a film together, our relationship changes. There, of course, might be some of that Freudian element of the young girl liking the older man. But both of us know it might not be permanent. We could wander off in separate directions some day.''

Imagining the couple's on and off-screen relationship, we cannot help but draw images of Hitchcock and his misogynistic bouts with Tippi Hedrin and other blonde bombshells. But that is apparently far from the case. ''I usually assimilate my role and play it as best I can. If you can do that, Nic leaves you alone. I remember that he was a bit hard on Michael Emil in *Insignificance*, though. Michael was very uncertain about some of the scenes, saying he wasn't really an actor and often feeling frustrated. That's when Nic stepped in and gave him a push. Nic would literally grab Michael's mouth and make him smile when a scene called for it.''

If anything, much of their work together borders on collaboration. Roeg is open to many of her suggestions, so long as, in the end, ''he calls the shots.'' To summarize Russell's most memorable and harrowing experience, we must return to the *Eureka* trial where she has to remain stationary and mutter dialogue that many screenwriters would never take beyond the typewriter. ''Some think that scene was just a re-enactment of one of our domestic quarrels. There may be a little bit of that, but it's much more. That scene has a lot of metaphysical ideas Nic had probably been carrying around with him long before he met me. I can remember being very nervous at the time. I had studied the script; so the words ended up just flowing out of me the way I had memorized them. We had to go through it about five or six times, and one time the camera ran out of film in the middle of my speech. That was disorienting. But when it was finally over, the whole crew applauded.''

Though *Eureka* may seem to be her most demanding role, she still holds a torch for *Bad Timing*, which was her rite of passage. ''I was just twenty-two then, and the role left such an impression on me. We both felt an attraction towards each other at the time, especially once we started filming in Marrakesh. He let me explore this character Milena in *Bad Timing* and did not make me hold back. I was much younger and fresher then, and now his attitude towards me is changing as I get more mature. I think he might miss that younger self.''

Russell, who was born in San Diego and grew up in California, had a turbulent post-sixties adolescence that involved the customary saturnalia of sex and drugs before being discovered by a photographer in a shopping mall. After a brief modeling stint, she left school to enter training at Los Angeles' Lee Strasberg Theater Institute. Shortly afterward, she had an affair with her psychiatrist who was twice her senior in preparation for that momentous occasion, sometime in 1978, when she locked horns with the Director. While the ''great, huge moment'' of their initial acquaintance has mellowed through time, Ms. Russell rejects the idea that the passion is over. ''I think my changes are forcing him to look at himself more differently. He likes to put his whole self into every film he makes. That's why he was so attracted to Jack McCann. Nic, in a sense, also feels that there is a lot of left-over life to kill. If anything, our relationship is just being re-defined.''

Regardless of whether she has exerted a positive or baleful influence, Russell's roles are certainly out of the ordinary enough to make otherwise indifferent viewers pay more attention to Roeg's gift for conveying character quirks. In *Track 29*, when she plays a sexually frustrated wife visited by a supposedly illegitimate son her own age, we are not surprised to find her adapting to the role as a matter of course. ''I guess you could call *Track 29 Bad Timing*'s next logical step. I play Linda, who is supposed to be a funny, off-the-wall character. The original script was much more brutal before Nic helped to change it. Instead of getting raped by the boy, I am seduced. Also, we take out a reference to me killing a baby.''

As befitting their ideal marriage-career contract, Russell often acts as a support system during Roeg's more desperate hours. This is true especially after *Eureka* was so cruelly received. ''*Eureka* is really Nic's gem. That's why it was such a blow to him when it was ridiculed and never released. He went into a deep depression after *Eureka*. I was pregnant with Stanton at the time. It was the one film he felt completely connected to, and no one wanted it. So, I can understand why he'd be wary of going back into a dark corner. After all, if nobody gets it, what's the point?''

Suddenly our conversation (partly in-person; mostly by telephone) is aborted by another child, their youngest, Max, screaming in the background. Once again, the Actress transforms into the Mother. As we leave Mother Theresa to don the apron and Father Nicolas to prepare another filmed chronicle on battles between the sexes, we can only wonder what their one dream film—an adaptation of Paul Bowles's novel *The Sheltering Sky*—would have been like if Bertolucci had not already gotten the option and Roeg was allowed to pursue Bowles's eschatology of married existence to the finish.

THE ELECTRIC BED

As lines so loves oblique *may well*
Themselves in every Angle greet:
But ours so truly parallel,
Though infinite can never meet.
—Andrew Marvell, "The Definition of Love"

Can the angle between two walls have a happy ending?
—J. G. Ballard

ROEG: What drew me to *The Man Who Fell To Earth* is a real story that happened to a friend of mine who was with the Egyptian Army. He had a nice family and was well situated, but he had to leave Egypt after Farouk was overthrown and everything changed. He went to America and had to leave the wife and children behind. He lived in New York City virtually as a beggar until he got himself an accountant's job. During his seven year stay, he eventually lost touch with his family and developed a relationship with this woman. Then, his wife traced him and implored him to get her and the kids out of Egypt. At that point, he had to make the decision. The night before his family arrived in America, he left the woman, and the pain he went through was incredible. Mr. Newton reminds me of that special person who got away and left someone behind. We can say the same about Claude in *Eureka*.

That explains why both films have so much melancholia.

Melancholia is a big part of every relationship. We all have a chorus of violins in the back of our minds whenever something like that happens to us. The idea of falling in love is a very recent innovation. Very much a western idea. The trouble with traditional marriage is that most people lie about themselves. The characters in *Castaway* travel 12,000 miles and take themselves with them. Marriage is a strange thing. It can really finish a relationship. I can name four people, one the head of a studio, who lived with someone for years and left them a few months after marriage. Marriage is like going to court. The average person is very reluctant about facing other people with a lie. It's like a couple who make love in a haystack. When the guy is finished, the woman taps him on the head and says, "By the time you've fucked me to death, I would have smashed your brains in with this piece of straw."

I like the way you equate marriage with penal servitude. Love and criminology. Tracy refers to love as an electric bed, replacing the electric chair.

It can be sheer torture, especially when the pretenses have to be removed. A relationship is usually about knowing nothing. The problem is magnified in *Castaway*. It's twenty years of marriage concentrated into one year. Hiding is what keeps a relationship going, and these people have no place to hide. Each day is a month, each month a year. There is also the fear of loneliness that, I think, came across well in Kubrick's *The Shining*. It wasn't a horror film so much as one about a faulty relationship that they try to mend by snowing themselves in an empty hotel. That is far more horrible than ghouls or vampires.

Sex and death are really one now.

Well, with AIDS, everything has changed. I recently met this woman whose lover of the last three years was an entrenched homosexual about five years before they met. The awful thing is that AIDS has come between them. She's the first person I've spoken to about the subject who admits she's scared shitless. Their break-up isn't going to be out of infidelity, but out of pure self-interest. Health has come before everything. The ramifications of that are huge. Hetero- and homosexual affairs are in total jeopardy. AIDS seems so contrary to nature that perhaps it is man-made. Nature is hard and harsh, but it isn't that cruel. There are even freak cases when cancer can go into remission. Even syphilis could burn itself out. But AIDS attacks life's source. I'm baffled by the disease. What is the message? It might be more simple than we can imagine. It may be about movement of populations. Bulks of people shift back and forth around the world. It may be a bit of a shock to nature. *Castaway* is, in many respects, a post-AIDS film. All that's left to love are the rituals. Now you have to lay out your cards beforehand. When someone wants to go out with you, you have to examine their advert more carefully.

With Castaway *especially, your career seems to have drastically changed. After* Eureka, *did you consciously decide to take a different turn?*

(*A long, silent pause.*) I guess I'm not likely to put everything I feel so easily observable on the screen. It's there, but more intricately hidden. The surface is simpler. As you know, I was deeply saddened by what happened to *Eureka*. I don't know if you've ever read the essay by Edgar Allan Poe. I think it was the last thing he wrote. In a letter, he said, ''After 'Eureka,' I have nothing more to say or do.'' I'm sad about the film, but one lives on through any sadness. *Castaway* may seem like such a departure, but in many ways, it's simply a concentration of what I've been concerned about all along: relationships between people and the pain of not communicating. There are moments when I have to stop and ask myself if I am sure of my own situation. I could be home on a Sunday afternoon: Theresa takes the kids on an outing and I stay home; we could both be entering different lives and never know it. When you stop to fathom something like that, it's like being at reality's edge.

There are too many forces that keep relationships from working out. It's a lonely time for a lot of us. Were you ever able to make any kind of contact? Even with your own children?

I have six children, whom I love dearly, but I cannot say I have ever made that strong connection. Very few parents can. Not all families are Disney families, I guess. It's very curious that people some time ago thought in terms of "family movies." People would always ask, "Where are those family movies?" Where are those families?! That's the answer! When I was a boy, I used to go to the movies with my parents. But it's different today. Go on a family outing now and you're bored shitless. There was a point in England when studios tried to regenerate family movies and, of course, they flopped on their asses because the kids don't want to go. In *Track 29*, I deal with immaturity and how we are all destroyed by other peoples' opinions of us. I admit I'm immature, but so is everybody else. Just because someone is a brain surgeon does not make them any less childish. It's about infidelity of intent and how shattering it is to find someone you've known for a long time has been lying to you. Perhaps we lie to ourselves when we try to look back on some innocent past. It's all just a hollow image that disappears when you try to touch it. So, how could I possibly lie to my audience and pretend my characters *can* make that connection?

You take us to a point when it can almost happen; then you forge a rift.

There is never complete contact. Relationships go far beyond just sexuality. *Bad Timing* approached that truth. The detective almost gets Alex to confess to the rape but is interrupted. Whose crime was it, really? Actually, I had discussed with Garfunkel and Keitel what would happen if Alex had confessed. Ravishment is not really that much of a crime over there in those circumstances. I looked it up. In most cases, the worst charge would have been aiding or abetting a suicide. However, we all concluded that if Alex admitted to it, and that fusion was made between them, the detective would never have been able to get rid of Alex. He would be on the phone with him day and night. I think that nature forbids that kind of connection between people. When it happens, it's an aberration. You have to keep some kinds of distance. You can get close, but you finally discover you are trapped and alone.

It's like an author and his subject.

That's a strange symbiosis, isn't it? Critics can use their work to release their frustrations. The subject matter is just a catalyst for their self-analysis. The bulk of energy in the world right now is young people going to the movies, plays, looking at scripts, watching television. Many are being punched out of universities with English degrees, and why not? You look at a script and come to the conclusion you can write just as well. People may need to over-analyze something because they secretly want to take it to bed with them. The boundary between you and your subject may seem delicate, but try to break through it and find out how much you are alone. Nobody knows jack shit about anyone.

The relationships in your films are all doomed; yet you cringe at any suggestion that you're a fatalist.

I never want to make a film without hope. I think of a wonderful story I heard years ago about a man chained in a cell. One day, after eighteen years, he realizes the chains are loose and yanks them from the wall. He breaks free, then comes upon an iron gate that is also loose. So he goes on into a long, dark tunnel. He comes upon another gate, pushes through, then sees a tiny shaft of light in the distance. He finally gropes his way into a smaller chamber full of light and sees two hooded inquisitors on each side of him as he enters. Suddenly, one of them says to the prisoner: ''I'm glad you haven't lost hope.'' Now he was able to go back and start on another eighteen years . . .

* * *

> *True love is what goes on and on, it never stops. Down and down into the water till you're drowning. And it's on the shore, in the sand, in the back of a car. And it's on the bed, it's an electric bed, isn't it? An electric chair switched on; neither of us can stop it. Shouting and shuddering. An electric bed on and on until you think you're dead.*
> —Tracy during *Eureka*'s trial scene

SOME FIFTY YEARS SINCE HIS CHILDHOOD TRAUMA AT Brighton Beach, Nicolas Roeg returns to the scene of his first cinematic apocalypse. Like the new generation of beachcombers, Roeg's science-fiction memory is lost in a cathode-ray haze. The only beach scene he can conjure is a banal image from a television ad: two distant lovers run toward each other in slow motion while a synthetic shoreline looms in the background. But instead of uniting, the couple keeps running in a loop, and the lovers never meet.

Roeg's labyrinths always lead to and never arrive at "love," a subject whose dubious simplicity gets increasingly wondrous and grotesque the more it is examined. This is not just the love between persons, but that protean exchange between the forces of nature and us creatures whom nature forever mystifies and abuses.

Like the seventeenth-century Metaphysical Poets, whose styles parallel his own, Roeg can only convey love's paradoxes and quagmires through harsh and often awkward metaphors. His craft is similar to what Roland Barthes refers to in *A Lover's Discourse* as an "image repertoire" which transposes our deepest feelings into a litter of conceptual abortions populating our fantasies long after the love object dissipates. Commemorating John Donne (famous for comparing a parting couple to the ever-widening legs of a compass), Roeg drains the flesh out of his romances to create a board game that exposes all erotic configurations as geometrically unsound.

> *The only way we can make contact with each other is in terms of conceptualizations. Violence is the conceptualization of pain. By the same token, psychopathology is the conceptual system of sex.*
> —J. G. Ballard, *The Atrocity Exhibition*

For Cinema's Hitman, the Electric Bed is a self-affirmation as well as a death sentence. He lulls us with the images, then imples that we should look away from the screen, re-enter our solitary lives, and at least try to rip open the latex body-suit or smash through the invisible plexiglass that blocks our touch. Hence, Roeg's greatest controversy is his handling of relationships and emotions. For some viewers, the passions are too overwhelming; for others, too flat. But Roeg, aware of this constant lack of resolve, acknowledges the inherent profligacy of trying to record human feelings with a camera. Again, Roeg echoes Barthes who, as a writer, confronts the same problem: "To try to write love is to confront the *muck* of language: that region of hysteria where language is both *too much* and *too little*." Roeg reminds us a bit of Michael Powell's possessed photographer in *Peeping Tom* who, knowing that his lens is impervious to love, concentrates instead on fear, making subjects view their contorted faces as a blade at the end of his tripod rushes to their throats.

Roeg forbids contrived sincerity. He would much rather destroy any potential intimacy with sudden cuts to isolated objects and body parts, or film characters from odd angles to give them an ominous bearing when they otherwise appear well-intentioned. In *Eureka*, as Helen reads aloud Tracy's overly sentimental letter, Roeg keeps switching his attention from her face to her jewelry: a flower dangling in the wind, or the stormy tide rising below their patio which will metaphorically sweep Jack into oblivion before the night ends. In *The Man Who Fell To Earth*, when Newton returns to his landing site for a nostalgic but painful moment, his submerged feelings surface in a close-up on his facial grimace, but the reflection in his sunglasses turns pitch black, and we are forbidden to get any closer. The same occurs in *Bad Timing* when Milena looks intently into her husband Stefan's deprived eyes while the camera prefers to shift to close-ups of their fingers lighting cigarettes or Milena's hand-shaped stick-pin—an image that reappears when Roeg hints that Milena subjects Alex to some playful S&M with a mannequin's arm.

The world of plastic objects and atmospherics often seems much more intoxicating than any misguided attempts his characters make to express themselves. In *Walkabout*, the children, especially the young woman, seem oddly indifferent to their father's death, just as Johnny, the Baxters' son in *"Don't Look Now"*, is more bemused than saddened to see his sister's lifeless body dredged out of the water. Perhaps this is the only fitting outcome for Roeg's excursions into time, "point of view," and identity. Operating on a schizoid strategy of overkill and neglect, he ameliorates the structuralists, post-Freudians, post-mods, supernaturalists and other professional paranoids who can at least wallow in sordid details and intellectual games when the film's emotional content goes bankrupt.

Roeg disturbs us because he is not afraid to admit that all lovers are frustrated vivisectionists. We are not satisfied until we pinion our object of affection, rearrange its body and mind, then discard it when we grow tired of answering our own questions. Movies are therefore the vivisectionist's panacea: to fall in love with a film star or cry during a love story is to harbor the illusion that all of our clichés are intact; that passion is still possible. This may be why Roeg adopts a Madame Tussaud approach to his characters, making them look more inanimate the closer they come to expressing what look like unfiltered sentiments. His stories simulate those telling moments at social gatherings when the background music stops, and we are left alone with our poses and the people around us with whom we are never really comfortable.

> *This trick of hers for expressing love by its unvarying and always perfect artifices began to make a dual impression on his mind. In its presence he was aware of the artifice. She seemed then to glow with love, a curious incandescence as unreal as it was effective. The glow was not of those mystic tapers which the heart kindles, but like an electric lighted advertisement of emotion . . . a thing that needed footlights, orchestra and a distance of twenty paces to seem genuine.*
> —Ben Hecht, *A Jew in Love*

By constantly centering on relationships only to reinforce their futility, Roeg continues to grind out cinema remakes of *Don Quixote*. The plots, decor and character combinations may vary, but the battle with false appearances is constant. Thinking again about some of his more quixotic vignettes, I can only recall pairs of disembodied eyes staring into each other: *Bad Timing* with Milena and Stefan on the bridge; *The Man Who Fell To Earth* as Newton and Mary-Lou reunite only to express their mutual numbness; *Insignificance* when The Actress sees her husband as another kind of alien; or in *Performance* as Chas and Turner finally realize they must sever their ties and retreat into separate traps.

And, as in *Eureka*, when Roeg neutralizes the emotions out of Tracy and Claude's final dinner party with a gushing string soundtrack, so does my own Muzak-laden dinner party with him achieve that sexless and listless mood ideal not only for his films but for every modern encounter. It is inevitable that my assessment of Roeg's travels along cinema's brink resists any pretense of objectivity. Unable to connect, I can only embellish. Just as Roeg may predicate his career on an elaborate misreading of both his audience and his own projected image, so am I left with nothing but perhaps my distorted self reflected in the image of Roeg that I want to see.

* * *

Well Nicolas, how does it feel to discover someone you thought you knew has a secret life?

It's inevitable. Everybody has one. Uncles, aunties, brothers, sisters—they don't know! And what is the greatest lover's question? Of any sex or race? "What are you thinking of, darling?" "I'm thinking about you, dear." But the truth is that you were thinking about something completely different. We're alone. I must get going, I'm afraid. It's been a very good chat. Hope it wasn't too muddled. I have a grasshopper mind. It leaps about a bit . . .

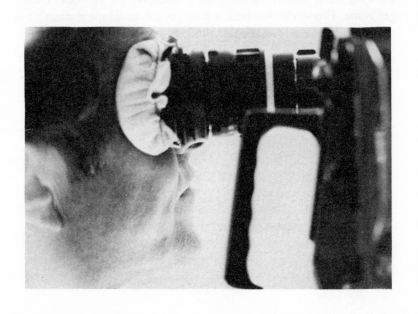

ROEG FILMOGRAPHY

SCRIPTWORK

(1961)
A Prize of Arms, with Kevin Kavanaugh
Dir: Cliff Owen
Great Britain
    Thriller about an unsuccessful attempt to steal an army payroll during overseas operation.

(1961)
Sanders
Dir: Lawrence Huntington
West Germany
    New version of Edgar Wallace's *Death Drums Along the River*. Diamond smuggling in an African colony, foiled by British Commissioner.

AS PART OF CAMERA CREW

(1950)
The Miniver Story
Dir: H. C. Potter
Great Britain

(1955)
Gentlemen Marry Brunettes
Dir: Richard Sale
U.S.A.

(1956)
Bhowani Junction
Dir: George Cukor

Pacific Destiny
Dir: Wolf Rilla

AS CAMERA OPERATOR

(1957)
The Man Inside
Dir: John Gilling

Island in the Sun
Dir: Robert Rossen

(1958)
Passport to Shame
Dir: Alvin Rakoff

A Woman Possessed
Moment of Indiscretion
The Great Van Robbery
The Child and the Killer
Dir: Max Varnel

(1959)
Jazz Boat
Dir: Ken Hughes

(1960)
The Sundowners
Dir: Fred Zinneman

The Trials of Oscar Wilde
Dir: Ken Hughes

AS LIGHTING CAMERAMAN

(1961)
Information Received
Dir: Robert Lynn

(1962)
Just For Fun
Dir: Gordon Fleming

Lawrence of Arabia (Second Unit)
(Train wreck sequence)
Dir: David Lean

The Caretaker
Dir: Clive Donner

Doctor Crippen
Dir: Robert Lynn

Nothing But the Best
Dir: Clive Donner

(1964)
Victim 5
Dir: Robert Lynn

Every Day's a Holiday
Dir: James Hill

The System (The Girl Getters)
Dir: Michael Winner

The Masque of the Red Death
Dir: Roger Corman

(1965)
Judith (Second Unit, Additional Photography)
Dir: Daniel Mann

A Funny Thing Happened on the Way to the Forum
Dir: Richard Lester

(1966)
Fahrenheit 451
Dir: François Truffaut

(1967)
Casino Royale
(Parachute and Bubble bath sequences)
Dirs: J. Huston, K. Hughes, V. Guest, R. Parrish, J. McGrath

Far From the Madding Crowd
Dir: John Schlesinger

(1968)
Petulia
Dir: Richard Lester

(1972)
Glastonbury Fayre
(Filmed record of Pop Festival held at Worthy Farm in June 1971)
Dir: Peter Neal

AS DIRECTOR

(1970; completed in 1968)
Performance
(Plus photography)
(Co-directed and scripted by Donald Cammell)
Warner Brothers

(1971)
Walkabout
(Plus photography)
(Special photography, Anthony Richmond; screenplay, Edward Bond; based on novel by James Vance Marshall)
Twentieth Century Fox

Luko's Diary (unfinished)
(Script based on exploits of Roeg's son Luc during filming of *Walkabout*)

(1973)
"Don't Look Now"
(Photography, Anthony Richmond; screenplay by Allan Scott and Chris Bryant; based on story by Daphne Du Maurier)
Paramount Pictures

(1974)
Deadly Honeymoon (never filmed)
(Screenplay, W. D. Richter; based on story by W. D. Richter)
MGM

(1976)
The Man Who Fell To Earth
(Photography, Anthony Richmond; screenplay, Paul Mayersberg;
based on novel by Walter Tevis)
British Lion-Cinema 5

Flash Gordon (never filmed)

(1979)
Bad Timing
(Photography, Anthony Richmond; screenplay, Yale Udoff)
Rank-W. W. Entertainments

(1982)
Eureka
(Photography, Alex Thompson; screenplay, Paul Mayersberg; based
on *King's X* by Marshall Houts)
MGM/UA

(1985)
Insignificance
(Photography, Peter Hannan; screenplay, Terry Johnson; adapta-
tion of Terry Johnson play)
Island Alive

(1986)
Castaway
(Photography, Harvey Harrison; screenplay, Allan Scott; based on
biography by Lucy Irvine)
Cannon Group

(1987)
King Zog Shot Back (from *Aria*)
(Photography, Harvey Harrison; based on Verdi's *The Masked Ball*)
A Miramar Films Release

(1988)
Track 29
(Photography, Alex Thomson; screenplay, Dennis Potter)
Island Pictures

(1989)
The Witches
(Photography, Harvey Harrison; screenplay, Allan Scott; based on story by Roald Dahl)

MISCELLANEOUS UNFILMED PROJECTS

Out of Africa (Based on novel by Isak Dinesen)
Hammett (Based on novel by Joseph Gores)
Miraclejack (Screenplay by Paul Mayersberg)
The Judge and His Hangmen (Screenplay by Paul Mayersberg)
Julia (Screenplay by Harold Pinter)
Victory (Based on novel by Joseph Conrad)
The Fan Club
The Voyage of Donald Crowhurst

SELECTED BIBLIOGRAPHY

Bad Timing brochure, from the 5th Hong Kong International Film Festival, 1981.

Ballard, J. G. *The Atrocity Exhibition.* Triad Panther: Great Britain, 1969.

Barber, Susan. "Bad Timing/A Sensual Obsession," Review, *Film Quarterly,* Fall 1981, pp. 46-50.

Baxter, Brian. "The Significance of Mr. Roeg," (Interview), *Films and Filming,* no. 30, July 1985.

Bloom, Harold, ed. *Selected Writings of Walter Pater.* A Signet Classic, New American Library: New York, 1974.

Borges, Jorge Luis. *Labyrinths: Selected Stories and Other Writings.* Edited by Donald A. Yates and James E. Irby. New Directions: New York, 1962.

_____. *A Personal Anthology.* Grove Press, Inc.: New York, 1967.

Callan, Michael Feeney. *Julie Christie.* St. Martin's Press: New York, 1984.

Colvin, Clare. "The Madness and the Ecstasy," *London Times,* February 5, 1983.

Combs, Richard. "Looking at the Rubber Duck: Nicolas Roeg talks to Richard Combs about working with François Truffaut on *Fahrenheit 451,*" *Sight & Sound.* Winter 1984-85, pp. 43-44.

Dunne, J. W. *An Experiment With Time.* 3rd ed. Faber & Faber: London, 1934.

_____. *The Serial Universe.* Faber & Faber: London, 1934.

Eagleton, Terry. *Against the Grain: Essays 1975-1985.* Verso, New Left Books: New York, 1986.

Eliot, T. S. *The Waste Land and Other Poems.* Harcourt, Brace and World, Inc.: New York, 1962.

Feineman, Neil. *Nicolas Roeg.* Boston: Twayne Publishers, 1978.

Fierberg, Steven. "Roeg on Roeg," *Lighting Dimensions.* Sept./Oct., 1987, pp. 56-74.

Fort, Charles. *The Complete Books of Charles Fort.* Dover Publications, Inc: New York, 1974.

"The 401st Blow: Seven on Truffaut," *Film Comment.* Jan.-Feb. 1985, pp. 42-43.

Fox, James. *Comeback: An Actor's Direction.* Foreword by Dirk Bogarde. William B. Eerdman's Publishing Company, Grand Rapids, MI, 1983. (First published Hodder & Stoughton Ltd., England.)

Gow, Gordon. "Identity: An Interview with Nicolas Roeg," *Films and Filming.* 18 Jan. 1972, pp. 18-25.

Gross, Larry. "Film Apres Noir," *Film Comment.* July-Aug. 1976, pp. 44-49.

Gussow, Mel. "Roeg: The Man Behind *The Man Who Fell To Earth*," *New York Times,* Aug. 22, 1976, II, 12.

Hodenfield, Chris. "Art Garfunkel's Real-Life Tragedy: A Case of Bad Timing," *Rolling Stone,* Oct. 30, 1980. Issue 329.

Holub, Robert C. *Reception Theory: A Critical Introduction.* Methuen: London and New York, 1984.

Houston, Beverle & Marsha Kinder. *Self and Cinema: A Transformalist Perspective.* Redgrave Publishing Co., Pleasantville, New York, 1980.

"Insignificance," *Monthly Film Bulletin.* Aug. 1985, vol. 52, no. 619. British Film Institute.

Irvine, Lucy. *Castaway.* Dell: New York, 1983.

Johnson, Terry. *Insignificance.* The Royal Court Writers Series, Methuen: London, 1982.

Kennedy, Harlan. "Roeg: Warrior," *Film Comment.* April 1983, pp. 20-23.

_____. "The Time Machine," *Film Comment.* Jan.-Feb. 1984, pp. 9-16.

Klein, Michael & Gillian Parker, eds. *The English Novel and the Movies.* Frederick Ungar Publishing Co.: New York, 1981.

Kolker, Robert Philip. "The Open Texts of Nicolas Roeg," *Sight & Sound,* 46 Spring, 1977, pp. 82-84.

"The Last British Filmmaker," (a screenplay/treatment by Tony Crawley), *Films Illustrated,* vol. 9, no. 106, July 1980, 391-396.

Lifflander, John & Stephan Shroyer. "Nick Roeg . . . and the man who fell to earth," *Andy Warhol's Interview,* 3 March 1976, pp. 34-36.

Lyon, Christopher, ed. *The International Dictionary of Films and Filmmakers: Vol. II—Directors/Filmmakers.* St. James Press, Inc.: Chicago, 1984, pp. 457-458.

"The man who fell on his feet (Derek Malcolm meets the latest white hope of British films, Nicolas Roeg)," *Guardian,* March 22, 1976.

Marshall, James Vance. *Walkabout.* Belmont Tower Books: New York, 1959.

Mayersberg, Paul. "The Story So Far . . . *The Man Who Fell To Earth.* A Commentary by the Screenwriter," *Sight & Sound,* Autumn 1975.

Milne, Tom. "*Eureka:* Interview with Paul Mayersberg," *Sight & Sound,* Autumn 1982, pp. 280-285.

_____. "*The Man Who Fell To Earth,*" *Sight & Sound,* 45 Summer 1976, pp. 145-147.

Norman, Neil & Davies/Starr. "The Face Interview: Nicolas Roeg," *The Face,* 1983, pp. 60-64.

Phillips, John (with Jim Jerome). *Papa John.* Dell: New York, 1986.

Polti, Georges. *The Thirty-Six Dramatic Situations.* Lucille Ray, tr. The Writer, Inc.: Boston, 1940.

Pulleine, Tim. "Nature's Call: Shooting Sun, Sand, and Sea in *Castaway,*" *Lighting Dimensions,* Sept./Oct. 1987, pp. 55-77.

Scharine, Richard. *The Plays of Edward Bond.* Associated University Presses: London, 1976.

Simon, John. "The Most Loathesome Film of All?" from *Movies Into Film.* The Real Press: New York, 1971, pp. 67-70.

Tevis, Walter. *The Man Who Fell To Earth.* Avon: New York, 1963.

Walker, John. "Rogue Talents: Nicolas Roeg and Ken Russell," from *The Once and Future Film (British Cinema in the 70s and 80s).* Methuen: London.

Waller, Nick. "Nic Roeg: Persistence of Vision," Riverside Studios pamphlet, 1978.

Wilson, Colin. *A Criminal History of Mankind.* Putnam Publishing Group: New York, 1984.

INDEX